Go West!

British adventures in Western China

By

Alexandra Needham

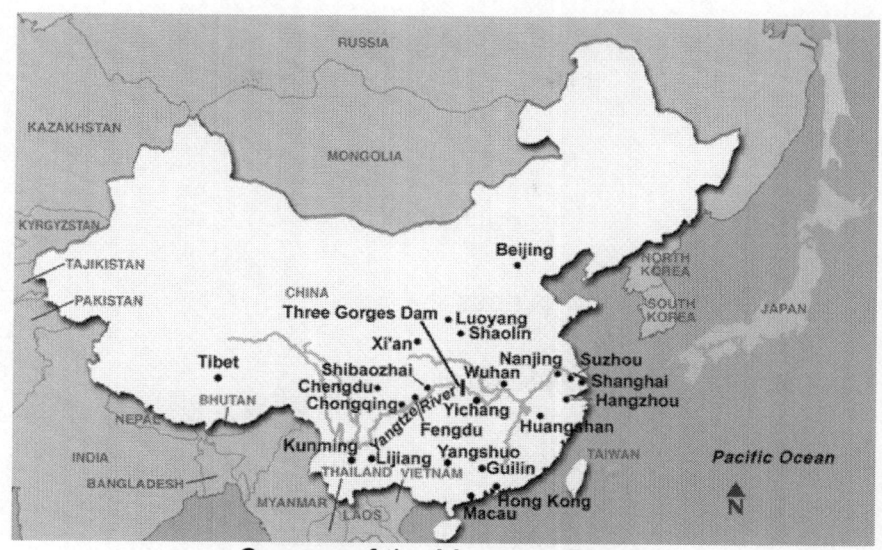

Course of the Yangtze River

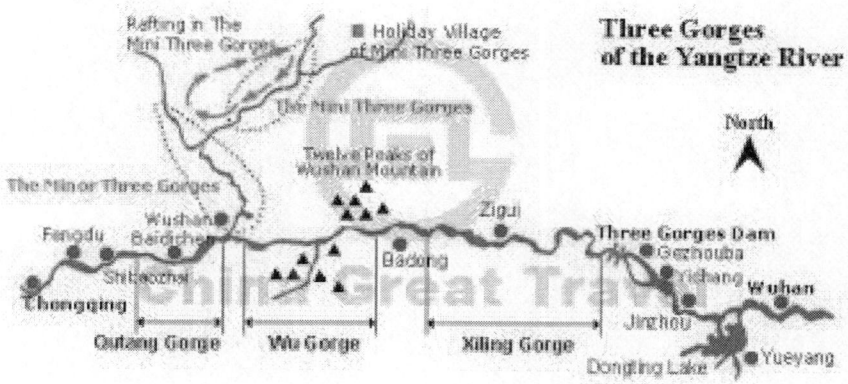

Map of the Three Gorges area of the Yangtze River, below
Chongqing

Contents

"In the Far Eastern and European press so much is heard of the awakening of China that one is apt really to believe that the whole Empire..is boiling for reform. But it may be that the husk is taken from the kernel. The husk comprises the treaty ports and some of the capital cities of the provinces; the kernel is that vast sleepy interior of China..

From Shanghai, up past Hankow, on to Ichang, through the Gorges to Chung-king, is a trip likely to strike optimism in the breast of the most sceptical foreigner. But after he has lived for a couple of years in an interior city as I have done, with its antiquated legislation, its superstition and idolatry, its infanticide, its girl suicides, its public corruption and moral degradation, rubbing shoulders continually at close quarters with the inhabitants, and himself living in the main a Chinese life, our optimist may alter his opinions, and stand in wonder at the extraordinary differences in the most ordinary details of life at the ports on the China coast and the Interior, and of the gross inconsistencies in the Chinese mind and character.

If in addition he has stayed a few days away from a city in which the foreigners were shut up inside the city walls because the roaring mob of rebels outside were asking for their heads, and he has had to abandon part of his overland trip because of the fear that his own head might have been chopped off..he may increase his wonder to doubt. The aspect here..--politically, morally, socially, spiritually--is that of another kingdom, another world. Conditions seem, for the most part, the same yesterday, to-day, and for ever. And in his new environment, which may be a replica of twenty centuries ago, the dream he dreamed is now dispelled".

Edwin Dingle, Across China on foot (1910)[i]

Chapter 1

<u>Introduction</u>

Between Marco Polo in the late 13th century and French priest Abbe Huc in the 1840s, practically no European set foot in western China – then considered one of the most difficult regions in the world for road, rail and river navigation given its formidable topography of high mountains, deep valleys and great rivers. This isolation gave western China somewhat of a reputation amongst westerners as a hidden El Dorado – a place of great wealth and fertility.

George Wingrove Cooke, The Times' special correspondent in Hong Kong during the second Anglo-China war (1856-8), summed up the West's 'great ignorance of China' as humiliating: "Even of that great conglomerate of cities on the Yangtze we know little more than that it is the commercial emporium of central China, and that its population is variously estimated at from five to eight millions of souls. We know that it exists, and that is nearly all we know. No one has been there except native Chinamen and Jesuit missionaries".

From the 1850s onwards, as the Victorian age was in full swing, Britons – and other westerners – began to develop a taste for overseas adventure, exploration and trade as the British Empire expanded its reach across the globe. Britain already had a strong hold in Hong Kong and was present in coastal treaty ports in China, but the Chinese market had not yet produced the massive increase in trade that many colonial expansionists had hoped for. A few adventurous souls began to believe that if access could be gained to the whole of China, through its inland ports, then access could be gained to the world's largest market with some 400 million people – the size of the whole of Europe.

This was not only access for trade purposes. Missionaries believed that the scope of the work they could do in inland China was endless, with a huge population most of whom had never heard of the word of God; and botanists and natural scientists wondered at the myriad exotic and as yet unknown species which flourished in China's sub-tropical south-western corner. Others were just curious and had an appetite – and the budget to match – for visiting foreign faraway lands and the challenge of the unknown.

Politically, opening up inland China was important to the British. Their aim was to develop a trade route from British India and Burma through China to British settlements in China's coastal cities such as Canton and Hong Kong, as part of the competition between western powers for influence in Asia known as the Great Game. The French in particular were Britain's adversaries for influence in western China, given the existing French stronghold in Indochina. French hopes were to reach the south-western Chinese province of Yunnan via the Mekong river through Vietnam, Cambodia and Laos.

On the basis of these dreams, hundreds of British travellers and explorers set their sights on the Yangtze River – the main access route to the heart and western regions of China – and in particular the region of Chongqing (then known as Chungking) in the western Chinese province of Sichuan – the biggest metropolis of western China. It was - and still is - a gritty inland city, worlds apart from the relatively cosmopolitan cities of China's eastern seaboard.

This book tells the story of their lives in this inland treaty port city, and surrounding region, from the 1870s to just after the Second World War when, for several years, Chungking served as the capital of China.

It details the achievements and lasting impact of the British in western China in the fields of diplomacy, trade, culture, science, education and religion. This includes introducing cricket and the first football match to the region; the printing press and the camera; the first steamship to sail through the treacherous Three Gorges – now tamed by the world's largest dam; and the inspiration for the longest book on China ever to be written in the English language.

The idea for this book came during my own time spent living in Chongqing from 2007 – 2010 as Political Consul at the British Consulate-General in the city. Chongqing was not the easiest of diplomatic postings. The curiosity of the locals, to whom the sight of a foreigner is a rarity, or just simply a bit of a laugh; the pollution; the fog and lack of sunlight; the difficulty of getting even the simplest things done; and incomprehension at every turn. Of course fascinating, but also very trying.

I started to wonder about the Europeans who came to Chongqing 150 years before me, and the city they must have experienced. In many ways the Chongqing of today still resembles a medieval city with its filthy winding alleyways and dark and dingy working class housing. The streets around my home in the port of Chaotianmen reminded me of scenes straight from Dickensian London, with migrant workers, men and women, scraping a living using their sheer body strength, from morning till night, carrying fridge freezers, flat screen TVs, boxes full of cheap trainers or whatever needed shifting for about 20p a load. At night they return to squalid dormitories, packed into decrepit tenement blocks with little lighting, ventilation or sanitation.

I became fascinated with the remnants of Chongqing's time as a Victorian treaty port and started to research the stories behind the derelict western-style buildings that remained. I spent weekends trudging through undergrowth on the South Bank of the Yangtze river and talking my way into decaying treaty port buildings, now home to families of migrant workers. I slowly began to piece together the stories featured in this book of Britain's contribution to the development of western China and British views of the world they discovered there, with the help of long-forgotten diaries and memoirs of former residents of the city.

Accurate descriptions of modern day China are hard to come by. Most fall into the clichés of the China of ancient, romantic traditions and dreamy landscapes; or the China of rampant economic growth ready to overtake the world with its dynamism. The same was true in the 19th century. A fashion for "chinoiserie" in Europe, fuelled by early explorations and a fashion for tea and Chinese silks and calicoes and other produce, led to distortions of the common view of China. This "Chinese myth" has lived on in many people's minds today.

The China I discovered when I went to live in Chongqing was not the China I had imagined. Where were the 5000 years of history? The historic temples and teahouses? Evidence of the harmony between man and nature so important to traditional Chinese culture? I am not denying that this does not still exist in some parts of the country, but in a city such as Chongqing they seemed wholly absent.

The people quoted in this book are rare because they shatter the myth. They talk of western China exactly as they saw it, warts and all. They describe so well the China I saw and the feelings it aroused in me. And they were writing about a China 100 – 150 years before the one I was witnessing, demonstrating that although China is in many ways changing incredibly fast, in places and in some ways it has not changed much at all in over a century. Their observations of Chinese society and culture present a remarkable record of China's past; and give a real feel of the juxtaposition of western society on an insular, and relatively backward Chinese city.

They are not always – or should I say not often? – complementary of what they saw, but today's reader should remember the context of Victorian society in which they were largely written. They also present, in some ways, remarkable similarities to life, seen through the eyes of foreign residents, in China's inland cities even today – a complete culture shock between east and west.

Of course, the British were not the only nationals to have contributed to the development of western China. There are other notable individuals who merit a mention in relation to this topic. These include German Ferdinand von Richtofen who did much to map and record the geological, geographical and economic wealth of China and is noted as coining the term "the Silk Road" to describe the ancient trade route from China to the west; and Hungarian Aurel Stein, known for his archaeological explorations of China and central Asia, who discovered an important cache of religious and secular documents in the Mogao caves of Dunhuang in the western Chinese province of Gansu which included the Chinese version of the Diamond Sutra which dates back to 868 and is, according to the British Library, the earliest complete survival of a dated printed book.

But the British were predominant in western China, particular in the early days of opening up the region to foreign trade, and considered the Yangtze River basin as their sphere of influence. This account stands as a testament to western China's British heritage and influence, lest it soon should all disappear amid China's rush to modernise and develop.

Chapter 2:

<u>Business</u>

"Building the Empire where there is an abundance of the straw wherewith to make the bricks, is a matter of no difficulty"

Edwin Dingle – Across China on foot (1910)

The early history of Britain's relations with China was one of a continuous struggle to open up and develop trade with a people who just weren't very interested, and largely content to keep themselves uncontaminated by the outside world. China has traditionally seen itself as the centre of the world: the Middle Kingdom. For much of its long history, China's engagement with the outside world was limited to trade with immediate neighbours, many of whom paid tribute to the Emperor. And for eighteen of the last twenty centuries, China had the world's largest economy. But in the mid-nineteenth century, Britain and other Western powers became intent on compelling China to conform with norms of international trade and diplomacy, confronting China's culture of self-sufficiency and cultural exceptionism head on.

The British East India Company was established by Royal Charter as early as 1600 to pursue trade with the East Indies. It came to concentrate its operations on pursuing trade with India and China, and had since the early 18th century turned a healthy profit. But it did so on humiliating and frustrating terms.

From the earliest days of the British Empire, Britain judged that, under the right conditions, the opportunities for trade with China were almost boundless, given its size and population. In the early 1800s, China ranked only 17th in terms of Britain's largest trading partners, on a par with Scandinavia. Britain's exports to China were only one-sixth of those to the United States which had a population of only 60 million.

British and other foreign traders (aside from the Portuguese who had had a foothold on Chinese territory in Macao since the 16th century) were subject to strict regulation by the Chinese Empire, which had set up a trading system that was controlled, stylised and within its own rituals. Foreigners were initially restricted to trading at the Chinese port of Canton (present day Guangzhou), which became the filter shielding the Chinese population in general and the Chinese officialdom in particular from disturbance by these foreign barbarians. Contact with foreign traders was maintained through a selected group of Chinese merchants – the Cohong – who operated both as brokers and superintendents of foreign trade. Further restrictions denied traders free access to raw materials and encouraged price-fixing and corruption. In addition, foreigners were not allowed to deal directly with shopkeepers, learn Chinese or keep Chinese servants. They were forbidden from permanent residence and denied access to the city of Canton itself, being restricted to a narrow area of shoreline on the edge of the city. Such restrictions inevitably led to foreign frustrations with the Chinese authorities.

Nevertheless trade was good as British demand for exotic products such as silk, calicoes and tea were high: as the British empire grew, so did people's taste for the exotic. China in turn imported British woolens and Indian cottons. Tea imports soon became the largest single item in Britain's trading account. In 1783 alone, nearly 6 million pounds of tea were sold in London, providing the whole profit of the East India Company. Government-imposed duties on tea raised 10% of the total revenue of England. But such success left the Company with an increasing imbalance in trade: between 1792 and 1807, while Company exports from England to China were worth only £16.6 million, imports from China were valued at £27.15 million[ii]. The shortage of silver to pay for the tea imports forced the British to seek other commodities to compensate for the loss and to bring in a profit.

LORD MACARTNEY.
From a print by Schiavonetti, after a picture by H Edridge.

Lord MacCartney

Britain needed to do something to redress the balance. King George III, anxious to secure a footing in China, dispatched Lord MacCartney to Peking in 1793 to persuade the Chinese to liberalise trade and seek permission to establish a British trading port. The Emperor sent MacCartney back to the king with a letter: there would be no commissioner or Embassy in Peking. The Chinese government was simply not interested in trading with the outside world or prepared to accept the European idea of free trade.

A second measure – to grant licenses to private traders to export Indian goods that were, unlike British textiles, in demand in China to improve the trade balance – was more successful. Two Indian products, raw cotton and opium, found ready buyers in Canton. Although never directly involved in the sale of opium, which was banned in China by an imperial edict of 1729 as an illegal drug, the East India Company was responsible for most of its production in India, mainly for its medicinal value. The actual business of selling opium was conducted through private agencies.

Opium was known in China as a medicine and cultivated there, but not widely used. But the Chinese were quick to adopt opium for recreational as well as medicinal purposes, as the East India Company soon discovered. The number of shipments of opium in privately licensed ships grew fast – from 600 chests in 1750, to 5106 in 1816 and 23,570 in 1832, having a devastating effect on the local population. In the year 1928 alone, 1.9 million pounds (lb) of opium were shipped to China from India. The tax received on this opium was enough to pay for the East India Company's entire tea exports to Britain that year, amounting to nearly 45 million pounds' worth[iii]. It is estimated that between 1720 and 1806 the volume of trade between Canton and Europe doubled every 18 years. The balance of trade, once so unfavourable to the East India Company, had swung in the other direction, thanks to opium, and the amount of Chinese silver required to buy the drug was beginning to threaten the national economy.

In 1834, the East India Company's monopoly on trade with the Far East was ended by Parliament and the China trade was opened to the competition of dozens of British companies, who had been petitioning the government and lobbying members of Parliament for free trade for years. A marked increase in the number of private traders calling at Canton with cargoes of opium followed. Opium traffic had turned into the sole profitable business for some British companies in southern China, flooding the entire black market and, inevitably, becoming a major cause of concern for the Chinese Government. Aware that the increasing outflow of silver in payment for imported opium was endangering the Chinese economy, in 1838 the Emperor decided to take decisive action. He appealed to all smokers to hand in their pipes and opium and even reportedly addressed a letter to Queen Victoria begging her to stop the immoral trade and implying a halt to the export of tea and rhubarb if the opium trade didn't stop. The letter, perhaps never received, had no effect[iv].

The foreign traders refused to give up their opium, claiming that since they traded on behalf of others, it was not theirs to surrender. In March 1839, the Emperor called for the blockade of all foreign factories in Canton. After 6 weeks, 20,000 or more chests of opium were handed over to the Chinese authorities who proceeded to destroy nearly 3 million pounds of raw opium and wash it into the sea. This destruction of foreign property, as seen by the British government and the China merchants, was the trigger for the first Opium War, led by the most prominent of the China-based British merchants, William Jardine. The company he founded remains a dominant force in British trade with East Asia to this day.

The Treaty of Nanking, signed on 29 August 1842, signified the end of the first Opium War and opened an unwilling China up to foreign residence and trade. It stipulated the opening of the cities of Canton, Foochow, Amoy, Ningpo and Shanghai to foreign residence and trade and allowed the establishment of Consulates. It also ceded the island of Hong Kong "to be possessed in perpetuity" by Queen Victoria and her successors.

British parliamentarians were at times surprisingly frank about the opium trade in China and British traders' prominent role in it: "If the Chinese must be poisoned by opium", said Sir George Campbell in the House of Commons in 1880, "I would rather they were for the benefit of our Indian subjects, than for the benefit of any other exchequer".

The Treaty Port era

This period marked the real beginning of Britain's expansionist plans for China: as trade grew, the possibilities of opening up the whole of China to British interests became somewhat of an obsession for British parliamentarians, businessmen and others. From 1843 onwards for the next 100 years, firstly in Shanghai and then later elsewhere along the coast and inland, treaty ports were created as a vehicle for British and other western interests in trade, diplomacy and evangelism, and established in the face of Chinese opposition. Russia, Germany, France, Italy, America and Japan all held territorial concessions in China, but Britain dominated numerically and led the way in the administration of the treaty ports.

Shanghai was the gateway for foreign traders coming to make their fortune in China, and by far the most important of the treaty ports, handling the majority of British trade. In 1843 it had a foreign population of just 100, of whom 7 were women. In 1850 this had grown to 175, not counting sailors. Far greater though than the increase in population was the number of foreign vessels calling at the port of Shanghai: 44 ships arrived there in 1844; by 1854 this had grown to 437 ships per year.

Shanghai sits at the mouth of the Yangtze River which flows through the heart of China and the major silk and tea-producing regions, but is also far enough from the sea to be protected from coastal typhoons. Its advantageous position in terms of trade was noted as early as 1756 in an East India Company report. In that year an exploratory mission aboard the Lord Amherst sailed into Shanghai to report on conditions for trade. Unable to get an audience with local trade officials, the British crew took to counting the number of junks on the river instead, thus forming an opinion of the prospects for the British woollen trade in the cooler western provinces accessible via the Yangtze: "Considering the extraordinary advantages which this place possesses for foreign trade, it is wonderful that it has not attracted more observation", the report notes.

The first British Consul, George Balfour, arrived in Shanghai in November 1843 and established a British consulate in the house of a wealthy local merchant. One of Balfour's first duties was to settle arrangements for the land allocated for foreign residence – in the case of the British, an area between the walled city and Soochow creek to the north. Like most of the land given over to foreign settlement in China, the land was vacant ground and covered with mulberry trees, cotton fields and ancestral graves. The land was leased "in perpetuity" from the Chinese by payment of a nominal land rent. British companies erected their headquarters and set about establishing trading links.

Banking houses soon followed to facilitate trade including the Oriental Banking Corporation, Mercantile Bank of London, India and China and Agra Bank, all established in 1854, and the Hong Kong and Shanghai Bank (HSBC), founded in Hong Kong in 1864. Businessmen were soon followed by their families, missionaries and other adventurers creating a vibrant foreign community. The city's heady mix of western decadence and oriental poverty and squalor is now the stuff of legend.

Though the Treaty of Nanking (1843) was followed by further treaties with the Americans and French, which extended the provisions of the British treaty, British merchants remained unsatisfied with their access to the Chinese market. The opening of the coastal treaty ports had not led to the vast expansion in trade that they had hoped for.

A Manchester Chamber of Commerce report in 1850 complained that the government of China *"endeavours in secret and indirect ways to oppose itself to the introduction of foreign manufactures by encouraging native jealousies and screening native aggressions...The strictly enforced limitation to five places on the seaboard prevents the growth of better personal feeling between the races and keeps concealed the causes of our stunted trade with China". The report went on to express "disappointment universally felt in respect of the results expected from the Treaty of Nanking and the "mistake made in limiting the right of ingress to five coastal ports".*

Britain's Eldorado: western China

From the 1850s onwards, British opinion started to gather pace that if only access could be gained to inland China, then access could be gained to the world's biggest market with some 400 million people and Britain would, more than it already did, rule the world and prosper. Given the limited accessibility of western China, surrounded as it was by high mountain ranges and accessed only by treacherous and as yet unnavigated rivers, little was really known about it aside from snippets from intrepid European explorers to the region. This only helped to heighten the area's mystique and appeal.

Marco Polo had described the riches of western China as long ago as the 1300s. He is reported to have travelled through the province of Sichuan, which he refers to as "Sindafu" which he described as "on the confines of Manzi (Thibet), and the capital city of which is also called Sindafu" – a land of great abundance. But his stories gained no credence for over 600 years until their remarkable general accuracy was demonstrated by Colonel Yule in a retelling of Marco Polo's travels in the mid 1800s.

To Britain's politicians, businessmen and the informed public, western China's huge population, the richness of its soil, its genial climate, inexhaustible mineral wealth and the untiring industry of the Chinese people presented an opportunity that they just could not resist. They began to push to open up more treaty ports in inland regions. The image of western China as an Eldorado for British trade was fuelled by reports from Consular officials and visiting trade missions describing the prospects for trade, sometimes in hyperbolic terms.

A Shanghai Chamber of Commerce report on exploration of the Upper Yangtze in 1869 speaks of the enormous potential for trade with inland cities such as Hankow:

"Its success as an emporium of trade has been sufficiently great to justify the opinion that trade with China can be extended to almost any amount, if European enterprises were allowed to invigorate and stimulate that of the natives". *Lord Curzon claimed in parliament in 1898 that "the opening of the internal navigation on all rivers in China to British steamers from the ensuing summer means that we shall be able to take British merchandise in British ships, not merely to the ports recognised by Treaty, but to every riverside town and station in the whole of the interior of China."*

A consular officer in China said in 1899 that "The three rivers, the Min, the Fou, the Yang-tse above Chung King, are in the most promising undeveloped commercial area in China, perhaps in this world, and I feel sure that it is only the general ignorance of foreign goods and the extreme difficulty of getting them, that prevents a largely increased consumption.”

Of Guizhou, which today remains China's poorest province with an average per capita income of just USD 3100, Consular official Alexander Hosie writes: “All that Kweichow requires to make it one of the richest provinces in the nation is population; cereals are so cheap that it does not pay to grow them.” In the same report he says of Yunnan: “The whole country seems alive with caravans – men, women, ponies, oxen and donkeys!ᵛ”

The city of Chungking was regarded as the ultimate goal of colonial expansionists for several reasons. It was the main commercial metropolis of the “Sindafu” referred to by Marco Polo and lay on the mighty Yangtze River, at that time the chief means to gain access to inland Chinese markets. It lay

1500 miles from the mouth of the river and therefore it was considered that if trade could be established freely, this would open access to the chief network of waterways in this vast country. Hence free trade with Chungking meant, in the dreams of colonial expansionists, free access to the majority of Chinese. In the words of one resident British consular agent, if this gritty metropolis could be opened as a treaty port, it would "create another Shanghai in western China, such are the ascertained riches of the Great West, of which Chungking is the key"[vi]

Finally, Chungking presented a major technical challenge, situated above the formidable Three Gorges. Here the riverbed was dotted with hidden rocks and powerful eddies and whirlpools rapids that had hampered and curtailed unhindered movement of goods for centuries. In many sections boats had to rely on teams of native trackers to haul the boat through the gorges with ropes tied around their bodies. The crews of descending vessels had to cope with such a rush of water that many ships ran out of control and foundered. A typical journey between Yichang and Chungking by this method took on average just over a month upstream and slightly less downstream. At the height of Britain's industrial revolution there was nothing like a technical challenge, a feat of man over nature, to further excite the interest of Britain's most intrepid adventurers.

Experts estimated that at that time trade with western China was less than a tenth of what it should be. So limited was foreign trade with western China in fact that there was a surplus of exports over foreign imports of over 40%! Those exports included silk and silkworm cocoons, drugs and white wax, salt, silver ingots and pig bristles.

Britain's interest in western China must also be seen through the prism of the Great Game – competition between European powers to divide up the world into areas under their influence. By the 1880s, European powers were looking at China as fruit ripe for the picking: the Russians pressed in from the north, the French from Indo-China in the south, and the British and later the Germans and Japanese, along the east coast and up the Yangtze.

The British saw the French in particular as their rivals. The French were making in-roads into Yunnan in the south-west of China from their base in Indo-China. Britain's annexation of Upper Burma in 1886 more than doubled the size of British Burma and made it contiguous to both British India in the north-west and China in the north-east. The British now claimed suzerainty over the Shan states – the southern part of Burma which shaded uncertainly into the Lao states – and thus took a giant stride into a part of inland south-east Asia on which French sights were already set.

France repeatedly concentrated its efforts on investigating the navigability of the Mekong river in the late 19th century, also viewing it as an important potential trade route from south-east Asia into the untapped market of western China, and Yunnan in particular. The success of the Lagree – Garnier Mekong River Commission in 1866 - 68 of mapping the majority of the Mekong river basin is particularly noteworthy. While concluding that the Mekong river was not indeed navigable between French strongholds in Indochina and Yunnan, the Commission discovered an alternative route into western China via the Red River which flowed into the Gulf of Tonkin in French-controlled Vietnam.

Britain believed it could counter French influence in western China and open up a trade route across China from British-controlled India and Burma across western China and into Hong Kong and Shanghai. This land route into China from India was shorter than that by sea into Canton and Hong Kong and seemed to offer many benefits to British and Indian merchants in both India and Burma. After all, India was the source of most of China's foreign imports - cotton and opium in particular - and much of British policy in the Far East was concerned with maintaining and extending this trade.

While their compatriots in China looked on neighbouring

Szechwan as the El Dorado of the East, the British in Burma and India had their eyes on the province of Yunnan. The extravagant and over enthusiastic appraisal of Yunnan's potential wealth gave rise to what became known as the "Yunnan Myth". By 1850, the possibility of extending trade from Yunnan into Szechwan was envisaged, and the glowing prospect of an extensive market for British goods in West China became an obsession among many British officials and merchants in Burma and India.

Some commentators thought that British merchants based in the British territory of Hong Kong were particularly well placed to benefit from the prospect of trade with western China. As Edwin Dingle puts it:

"The whole of the trade of the three western provinces – Yunnan, Kweichow and Szechwan – has for all time been handled by Shanghai, going into the interior by the extremely hazardous route of these Yangtze rapids, and then over the mountains by coolie or pack horse. This has gone on for centuries. But now the time has come for the Hong Kong trader to step in and carry away the lion share of the greatly increasing foreign trade for those three provinces by means of the advantage the new Tonkin – Yunnan railway has given him".

He goes on to say: *"I think the railway is destined to turn the trade route to the other side of the empire. It is merely a question as to who is to get the trade – the French or the British. The French are on the alert. They cannot get territory, now they are after the trade."*[vii] However, despite a number of requests to enter China via other routes, the Chinese stuck to their guns, insisting that British access to China for trade purposes must be through Canton.

The key hindrances to developing a level of trade with the Chinese commensurate to their wealth, civilisation and size of population were considered to be the rudimentary condition of China's roads, the discouragement of mining and the multiplicity of inland tax stations run by provincial government officials with vested interests. There was also a sense – rather un-politically correct today – that the Chinese were lethargic and needed western help to develop their country:

"as one meanders through the country, watching a people who are equalled nowhere in the world for their industry, plodding away over the worst roads any civilised country possesses, he cannot but think, even looking at the question from the Chinese standpoint so far as he is able, that, were free scope once given for the infusion of western energy and methods into an active, trade-loving people like the Chinese,

China would rival the United States in wealth and natural resources.

The Chinese knows that his country, the natural resources of the country and the people, will allow him to do things on a scale which will by and by completely overbalance the doings of countries less favoured by Nature than his own. He knows that when properly developed his country will be one of the richest in the world, yet even when he is filled with such ideas he is just as cunctative as he has ever been. He has the idea that he should not commence to exhaust the wealth of his country before it is absolutely necessary"[viii]

So little was known about the geography and conditions of western China at the time that records show British and French explorers light-heartedly planning roads and railways through this mountainous and largely inaccessible region, when earth moving and other civil engineering techniques were primitive by modern standards. There was talk of building a railway through the Three Gorges from Yichang to Chongqing, as well as a proposal for a "Golden Railway" from Rangoon through Chiang Mai in Thailand to Yunnan, involving over a thousand kilometers of track through pestilential rainforest and around unstable mountainsides, which it was hoped would lead to *"fresh hands in the Manchester mills and growing activity on the Liverpool wharves"*[ix]

In fact, well into the 20th century, there was no wheeled transport to be found in western China except for wheelbarrows on the plains. Everything had to be carried, occasionally by horse or mule, but usually by coolies, along narrow paths winding up and down hills and through the paddy fields. Even in an age of "railway mania" and of government guarantees for railway investors, these were tracks too far.

The lengthy transportation requirements made the cost of most western products prohibitive. Added to that was the multiplicity of customs stations, which increased the further west one travelled.

On the 1000km stretch of the Yangtze river between Shanghai and Yichang goods were charged import duty just once. However, on the latter stretch into Szechwan there lay a dozen customs houses. Under the terms of the treaty with the Chinese duty was not payable at each of these but officials had the right to stop and examine transiting goods at their will. Duty was again payable on arrival at destination in Chungking.

These inconveniences and extra costs were a further barrier to trade: a Bradford Chamber of Commerce report on prospects for trade with Western China dated 1869 reports that wholesale prices in Chungking were a full 20% higher than in Shanghai as a result. The report states:

"every advance in price limits consumption in China, and the great problem for those who desire to extend trade in this particular locality is therefore how to reduce the expense of carrying goods from Hankow to Chungking. This is proposed to be done by establishing regular steam communication between Hankow and Yichang on a watercourse which presents no difficulties of navigation". It further concludes:

"if foreign ingenuity could be permitted to open a road through the 360 miles which divide Yichang from Chungking, either by steam on the river or by railway, the benefit to the Government and people of China would be enormous"[x].

The transport conditions for western goods meant that those that did arrive in country were often damaged in their final stages of transport as they were tossed by coolies from wagon to wagon and carried along rough country roads. Edwin Dingle writes:

"I saw coolies on the way to Yunnan-fu with German cartridges and Japanese guns, the packing, so different generally to British goods which come to China, being particularly good. This is one of the cries of the importer in China against the British manufacturer; and if the latter knew more of Chinese transport and the manner in which the goods are handled in changing from place to place, one would meet fewer broken packages on the road in this land of long distances. A friend of mine, needing a typewriter, wrote home explicit instructions as to the packing. "Pack it ready to ship," he wrote, "then take it to the top of your office stairs, throw it down the stairs, take machine out and inspect, and if it is undamaged re-pack and send to me. If damaged, pack another machine, subject to the same treatment until you are convinced that it can stand being thus handled and escape injury." This is how goods coming to Western China should be sent away"[xi]

A common view in the West at the time was also that the nature of the Chinese language and culture held back progress and the expansion of commerce. "If commerce in the Interior is to grow to any great extent in succeeding generations, warranting direct correspondence with the ports at the coast and with the outside world" writes Edwin Dingle, "the Chinese hieroglyph will not continue to suffice as a satisfactory means of communication. No correspondence in Chinese will ever be written on a machine such as I am now using to type this manuscript, and this valuable adjunct of the office must surely force its way into Chinese commercial life. But only when Romanization becomes more or less universal"[xii].

The Treaty of Tientsin and the Second Opium War

In 1854, the British government decided to press, with the French and Americans, for the renegotiation of the Nanking Treaty to include access to all of China (or at least the Chekiang coast and the lower Yangtze), legalisation of the opium trade (the only profitable British import to China), abolition of internal duties or levies on foreign goods in transit, and residence of a British Ambassador at Peking.

The Chinese authorities resisted renegotiation, but also continued to debar foreigners from entry to the walled city of Canton, considered to be contrary to the original provisions of the Treaty of Nanking. This, against a background of rising tensions, and an incident involving a British ship detained by Chinese authorities on suspicion of piracy in the waters off Canton, led to the Royal Navy being despatched to uphold British principles. British shelling of Canton quickly followed. In response the Governor of Canton placed a bounty on every English head, further restricting the activities of foreign merchants.

Further violence followed on both sides, in what became the Second Opium War. In January 1857, the Foreign Office authorised the Governor-general of India to send an artillery regiment to China, and in February it ordered Admiral Seymour to proceed to the Yangtze and blockade the Grand

Canal to try and starve Peking into submission by interrupting the imperial rice barges. The British government continued to press the Chinese for ambassadorial residence in Peking, more treaty ports and access to the interior.

In March 1857 a "special plenipotentiary", Lord Elgin was appointed to deal with British affairs in China. His brief was to take over the demands for treaty revision that had been unsuccessfully pursued by the British, Americans and French representatives in China. Arriving in Shanghai in 1858, Elgin spoke of some British merchants' attitude towards the Chinese market, which he felt denied important truths: "he felt that they must acknowledge China as a "laboriously manufacturing" society of considerable self-sufficiency, and that British trade would be increased not by the removal of trade barriers but by "proving that physical knowledge and mechanical skill, applied to the arts of production, are more than a match for the most persevering efforts of unscientific industry".

On 29 June, despite pressure from the Americans, French and Russians to abandon the demand for ambassadorial residence in Peking and permission to trade in the interior, (which they felt would be refused by the Chinese and might jeopardise their separate negotiations), the Sino-British Treaty of Tientsin was signed. It included the right to appoint an Ambassador to reside in Peking, protection by the

Chinese authorities of Protestant and Catholic missionaries, unhindered travel for British subjects on consular passports, the right of British ships to trade on the Yangtze River, the opening of more ports, an indemnity to be paid by the Chinese to compensate for "losses at Canton, and.. the expenses of war" and a fixed single charge on the transit of goods. The treaty was rapidly followed by American, French, German, Dutch and Spanish negotiations establishing the same concessions. Elgin had accomplished what he set out to do.

The Treaty of Tientsin had enormous consequences for China, long isolated from the West. Foreign missionaries and merchants could now travel freely throughout the country and both were officially to receive the protection of the local authorities wherever they went. And the Yangtze, which flowed through the western province of Sichuan and the tea and silk producing central provinces, was opened to foreign trade. New treaty ports were quickly established at the lower Yangtze towns of Chinkiang, Hankow and Kiukiang.

Later, in 1876, Yichang and Wuhu were reluctantly opened up to foreign presence by the Chefoo Agreement, pushing British influence along the Yangtze further inland.

This Agreement was a form of compensation for the murder of British consular official and explorer Margary in Yunnan. Margary had been on an official mission to greet a British mission from Burma on the border with Yunnan and escort them over the border into China. Margary was savagely murdered, reportedly at the instigation of the local Viceroy, despite Chinese government assurances that the British mission would be offered every assurance on the route. Yichang lay a further 400km inland from Hankow and although a poor mountain town, derived some importance from its position on the edge of the fertile and coal-rich Sichuan basin.

Chinese negotiators also agreed to allow British warehouses and commercial establishments in Chungking, thus constituting it as a Treaty Port, under the stipulation that such permission would only take effect when steamships succeeded in ascending the Yangtze up to Chungking. Chinese negotiators may have felt they had scored a cunning success against the foreign barbarians, as they were reasonably certain that the ascent would be far beyond the capabilities of the foreigners; strange machine-propelled ships. But the British negotiating team had much more faith in steam engines.

It fell to Japan, after the war of 1894-5 to claim the right of steam navigation to Chungking, and by article VI of the

Treaty of Peace signed at Shimonoseki on 17 April 1895 not only was Chungking opened to the trade, residence, industries and manufactures of Japanese subjects, but steam navigation for vessels under the Japanese flag for the conveyance of passengers and cargo was extended on the Upper Yangtze from Yichang to Chungking. By a most-favoured nation clause, therefore, Chungking was opened to foreign trade on the same conditions as the other Treaty Ports in China.

Early Chungking residents

Archibald Little

By the late 1880s, a handful of intrepid Brits had already established themselves permanently in Chungking for purposes of trade.

Chungking's first foreign resident was British entrepreneur Archibald Little, whose name is synonymous with efforts to bring the resources of western China within reach of European traders. Archibald Little was born in London in 1838, the son of a medical doctor. He was educated at St Paul's school and in Berlin.

In 1859 he moved to China where began a lifelong association with China and its people. He began work as a tea taster for a German company in Shanghai and then later moved westwards to Yichang, then Chungking, where he founded the Chungking Trading Company in 1887 and dabbled in many aspects of trade, brokering and insurance.

Amongst Little's enterprises was a factory which cleaned and sorted pig bristles for export – for use in products such as household brushes because of their highly abrasive characteristics. Chungking bristles became a well-known export, thanks to Little, and the business remained successful until 1912, when a local group of Chinese set up their own bristle-exporting company which proved more competitive.

Little also operated the Kiangpelting Mining Company in Szechwan, known at the time as the *"best coalmine in the world after Cardiff"*. He also appears to have operated a monopoly on land located along the south bank of the Yangtze in Chungking where most foreigners settled, leasing land, amongst others, to the British government for the site of the Embassy building, for GBP 15 per annum, and to shipping company MacKenzie and Co.

It appears Little was viewed as difficult and not well liked amongst British consular agents at the time, due to his tenacious approach to pursuing his business interests. British Consular agent Sly is reported to have remarked of Little and his partner: "..in their case Chinese cunning is dished up with European duplicity and chicanery, a consomme which is bad to the taste[xiii]."

Aside from these commercial interests, Little was at heart an explorer and inventor who dreamt of taking a steamship through the Yangtze Three Gorges – a feat never before achieved – in order to open up the immense possibilities for trade he saw in Szechwan province and beyond, in Tibet.

Little first tried an ascent of the Yangtze from Shanghai to Chungking by Chinese junk in 1883, which he records in detail in his book "Through the Yang-tse Gorges or Trade and Travel in Western China" (published in 1888) - a journey of two months. Little describes some of the difficulties of navigation in the Three Gorges as follows:

"A big junk of 150 tons carries a crew of over 100 men, viz. seventy or eighty trackers, whose movements are directed by beat of drum, the drummer remaining on board under the direction of the helmsman; a dozen or twenty men left on board to pole, and fend the boat off the boulders and rocky points as she scrapes along, and also to work the gigantic bow sweep formed of a young fir tree. Another half dozen of the crew are told off to skip over the rocks like cats, and free the tow-line from the rocky corners in which it is perpetually catching; besides a staff of three or four special swimmers called "tai wan ti" or water trackers, who run along, naked as Adam before the fall, and may be seen squatting in their haunches on rocks ahead, like so many big vultures, prepared to jump into the water at a moment's notice and free the tow line, should it catch on a rock inaccessible from the shore. These tow lines are made of strips of bamboo plaited into a cable as thick as the arm, and which require great skill in coiling and uncoiling, which is incessantly being

done, as the necessities of the route require a longer or shorter line.

Notwithstanding its enormous toughness, owing to constant fraying on the rocks, a tow line only lasts a single voyage, and when one sees deep scores cut by the tow lines into the granite rocks along the tow path, the fact is readily accounted for. The trackers of our humble craft stripped themselves of everything but one jacket, being in and out of the water all day long, and, as it was, we at times caught the tow line, when the boat would drift back on the rocks before it was freed again; but we managed to start ahead again just in time to avoid incurring serious damage"[xiv]

Little also describes other boats less fortunate than his own in their ascent:

"Aided by a fair wind, we ascended the T'ung-Ling rapid, which intervenes between these two gorges, without difficulty, but the channel at this period is strewn with rocks, and the navigation requires great care. It was here that in September last, the wealthy general Pao-Chao, the T'i-Tu or commander-in-chief of Hu-Peh province (which we are now in) was wrecked, proceeding upstream, through the junk's tow line catching in a rock simultaneously with a sudden failure of the wind, which otherwise might have enabled the junk to steer clear of the danger.

His two sons and several of his suite were drowned by the capsizing of the junk in the whirlpool, and he himself was only rescued by the life-boat, one of which, as before mentioned, is stationed at the foot of each rapid."[xv]

Already in this work Little talks extensively about the possible use of steamships on the Upper levels of the river. However, an ascent by steam was not to be attempted until some full 15 years later, again by Little himself.

The Times reported at the time that *"Mr Little's expedition will be watched with great interest; if his bark does not carry Caesar and his fortunes, it carries a large part of the fortunes of British trade of the future with one of the largest and wealthiest of the unopened markets of the world"*[xvi].

Little had the steamship SS Kuling built on the Clyde and shipped out to Shanghai in pieces and reassembled there. Having made good progress up the Yangtze to Yichang, the SS Kuling encountered trouble. It was detained by Chinese officials and prevented from going any further upstream as according to the Chefoo Convention of 1876 Chungking would only be declared an open port to international trade once a steamship had reached there, and Chinese steamships had to be the first to ply this section of the river.

It was not until after the Sino-Japanese War and the Treaty of Shiminoseki in 1895 that this restriction was abolished.

Little ended up selling the "SS Kuling" to Chinese owners at a vast profit and it traded on the Yangtze up to Ichang for many years, but never beyond.

Little was not disheartened though. He travelled to Britain where he spoke widely to Chambers of Commerce in order to garner financial support for a second attempt to ascend the Gorges. Although his mission incited great interest from parliamentarians and business alike, little money was forthcoming and Little ultimately financed the building of a new 50 foot Yangtze steamer, the Leechuen, himself, at a cost of £10,000.

The ship was build by Denny's of Dumbarton, shipped to Shanghai in pieces and then reassembled. Eight years after the opening of Chungking as a Treaty Port, Little made a successful ascent of the Yangtze from Yichang to Chungking by steamboat in 3 weeks, arriving triumphantly in Chungking on 3 March 1898. Little's arrival in Chungking was greeted by Union Jacks, three cheers and songs by a small jubilant party of resident English and Americans[xvii].

In 1900, the river gunboats HMS Woodcock and HMS Woodlark repeated the trip. Archibald Little had not been idle, however, and later that year he navigated a large paddle steamer he had built, SS Pioneer, on the same journey.

Soon thereafter SS Pioneer was commandeered by the Royal Navy in order to evacuate Europeans from Chungking during the Boxer Rebellion (97 Europeans and 60 Chinese were successfully rescued). The Pioneer was found to be such an excellent vessel that the Royal Navy purchased her in 1901. Renamed HMS Kinsha, she became the Royal Navy Yangtze flagship until 1921, when she was replaced by HMS Bee.

Writing in a Royal Geographical Society publication in 1901 Little sets out the possibilities of establishing a permanent steamboat service through the Yangtze Gorges:

"One thing our summer voyage on the upper Yangtse definitely impressed upon us, and that is that a permanent and profitable steam-service is simply a question of supplying the needful capital for suitable boats. Is this navigation to lie carried on or to be abandoned to others by the British, who have been the first to successfully attempt it? In any case, we reached Wan Hien, fourteen days out from Ichang, with the firm conviction that this would prove our last ascent of the upper Yangtse in a Chinese junk".

Thanks to Little's pioneering efforts, by 1910, the journey from Yichang to Chongqing could be made in just 9 days by steamer. By 1925, the trip took just three and a half days upriver and one and a half days down.

But travel by night, even at this time, was still considered to be too dangerous and insurance companies refused to cover it. Only after 1931 was night sailing considered safe enough to insure. By the mid 1920s an average of 30 trading steamers a week were reaching Chongqing and the wash from these high-powered boats frequently capsized overloaded junks who were struggling to compete with the new ships. By the end of the 1930s there were over 70 passenger/cargo steamships on the Upper Yangtze, although banditry by pirates was not uncommon.

Over the years, a sustained programme of dynamiting the more hazardous rocks along the Three Gorges area has eliminated the most dangerous rapids and obstacles en route. And since the construction of the Three Gorges Dam, navigation is much easier given the increase depth of the upper sections of the river. These days, ships carrying over 1000 passengers, the majority crammed into 4th and 5th class berths, ply the 2400 kilometre journey from Shanghai to Chongqing, taking just seven days upstream and five days back.

Archibald Little will go down in history as the Englishman who proved it was possible to navigate the Three Gorges by steamship, thus transforming trade patterns in western China. But he also left behind him a whole body of literature on the interior of China and Tibet. During his time in Chungking, he travelled extensively with his wife Alicia. His works include " Mount Omi and Beyond" (1901) describing his travels overland through Sichuan to present day Emei Shan (Emei mountain), "Across Yunnan" (1910), "Through the Yang-tse Gorges, Or, Trade and Travel in Western China (1888) and "Gleanings from Fifty Years in China" (1910).

On top of that, Little played an important role in urging the British government to assert its predominance in China, protecting British trading interests against Russian and German competition, and forcing commercial and industrial reforms on the Chinese. He argued vocally that more liberal mining and industrial laws would lead to almost unlimited investment of foreign capital in China, and this would lead to the upskilling and improved employment situation of local people. He also assisted many of his wife's social reform efforts, including the anti-footbinding movement which will be described in more detail in Chapter 4.

British trading with western China

The establishment of a British Consulate and an office of the Chinese Imperial Maritime Customs at Chungking in April 1891 rendered possible a more precise estimate of the capacity for trade of the provinces of the west of China.

In the 6 months from June – Dec 1891, 300 junks with a capacity of 7332 tons reported at the Foreign customs house in Chungking from Yichang, with foreign goods valued at 1.37 million Haikwan taels; while 307 chartered junks of a capacity of about 4404 tons left Chungking for Yichang, with exports of a value of 1.38 million Haikwan taels and silver valued at 84,381 Haikwan taels.

The trade steadily increased and in 1895 as many as 1200 junks transported nearly 37,000 tons of goods from Yichang to Chungking, 878 of which were chartered by the British, 112 by the Americans and 210 by Chinese merchants. Conversely, 917 chartered junks were carried away from Chungking loaded with native produce.

Writing from Chungking in January 1896, Mr. Woodruff, Commissioner of Customs wrote, in reference to the previous year's trade figures:

"Our petty share of the trade (ie: the trade passing through the Foreign Custom house) has prospered....With prosperity based on such uncertain foundations, it would be unwise to draw too definite conclusions, but there is enough else in the appended tables to give abundant promise: there are the possibilities of a great trade"[xviii]

The Customs Returns give precise details of the nature of this trade. Of the 6.39 million taels of exports reported at the foreign customs house in Chungking in 1895, native opium accounted for 2.87 million taels of this, ranked the number one export from the region. Commissioner of Customs, HE Hobson commented in a report in 1891:

" there is now little doubt that, with anything approaching a favourable season, the out-turn of the poppy fields of Western China alone are ample to the ordinary requirements of pretty nearly the whole Empire. It would be idle to attempt an estimate of the probable total yield of what is now the favourite spring crop of regions vaster in extent than individual European kingdoms; but the fact is patent that, as regards her opium supply, China is now practically "independent"[xix]

In order of importance, other native exports included white wax, silk, medicines, musk, sheep's wool, bristles, hemp, fungus, brown sugar, feathers, leather, safflower and turmeric. The principle foreign goods consumed by the Sichuanese were Indian cotton yarn, plain grey shirting, white shirting, Italian cottons, American clarified ginseng, cotton lastings, woolen lastings, analine dyes, long ells, seaweed and agar-agar.

But there were some concerns that consumption of western goods was not quite catching on as fast as predicted. Of British shirting, a consular report of 1893 reports: *"the country people complain that they do not give as much protection from the weather as the native cloth and that they will not stand their primitive style of washing, which includes placing the wet garments on a stone and thumping them with a club". But other products were surprisingly successful: "for the increase in woolen yarn... the curious reason is given that ladies have taken to using this yarn, dyed red, for binding their hair"*

British traders in Chungking

A number of British companies settled in Chungking for the purposes of trade. In addition to Archibald Little, these included Jardine Mathesons, Brunner Mond (later known as ICI), the British Salt Administration, MacKenzies and Swires. The names of other traders have unfortunately largely been lost to history.

The majority of these traders settled on the south bank of the Yangtze River opposite the main city of Chungking, away from the crowded, dirty streets, and traces of their presence can still be seen in the city today. Old photographs of this area show large western godowns (warehouses) lining the riverside with the names of the companies concerned emblazoned on their walls and roofs.

MacKenzie and Company

In 1847, William Mackinnon and Robert Mackenzie, formed the *Mackinnon Mackenzie Company* (MMC), a general mercantile partnership based in Calcutta which carried mail between Calcutta and Rangoon. A connection with China was made in 1868, in conjunction with the Messageries Maritimes of France. In 1919, MacKenzie and Company started a regular commercial service on the Upper Yangtze using the Loong Mow, a 196.5 feet long by thirty-one feet beam vessel built at the Kiangnan Dockyard in Shanghai. The twin reciprocating engines and oil-fired water tube boilers were built by Thorneycroft of Southampton, and the luxurious accommodation for both Chinese and foreign passengers led her to be called "The Queen of the Gorges".

This formed the start of regular shipping lines through the Yangtze Gorges. A Mackenzie and Co godown can be seen clearly on the waterfront on the south bank of the Yangtze in old photographs of Chungking from the early 1900s. MacKenzie and Company were soon joined by American Dollar Line ships and some small tankers of the Standard Oil Company; and in 1925 by several steamers of the Yangtze Rapids Steamship Company. For a time this latter company operated a through service between Shanghai and Chungking. French, Italian, and Japanese steamers also appeared at this time. By the end of 1925 there were at least thirty-two steamers on the Upper Yangtze—eight British, seven American, three Chinese, six French, five Italian, and three Japanese. The average journey time between Ichang and Chungking was cut to just three days, as against an average of a month by junk.

British Salt Administration

Records are scant on the precise history of the British Salt Administration offices in Chungking. In the 19th century, Liverpool had become the entrepot for much of the world's salt – and China offered vast salt reserves. The first mention of salt in China is found in the annals of the Emperor Yu dating BC 2205-2197, who ordered the province of Shantung to supply the court with that commodity. Sichuan province was one of China's biggest salt-producing regions. Sichuan was exploiting salt-well technology well before the Christian era including blast furnaces to smelt iron and steel bits able to bore holes up to a depth of 2,000 feet.[xx] In China salt was considered one of the seven necessities of everyday life, along with fuel, rice oil, sauce (in which salt is used), vinegar and tea.

Given this importance, and the large number of Chinese consumers, the salt trade was held as a monopoly by the Chinese government, with the country divided into circuits; price differentials varied greatly and customers were limited to buying from licensed dealers in their own area. Duty and taxes were levied at the depots and in transit; private salt-making forbidden and movement of salt from one circuit to another was regarded as smuggling.

As the commercial centre of Sichuan province, Chungking would have been of interest to colonialists interested in obtaining a share in China's vast salt wealth. Salt provided a steady, reliable income good enough to be accepted together with the rapidly increasing customs as security for the foreign loans needed to 'modernise' China. One of the most important, the Reorganization Loan for USD 25 million, was raised by Britain, France, Russia, Germany and Japan in 1913 with the proviso that a number of foreigners should be appointed to co-operate with the Chinese in the Salt Administration management and to see that the revenues were repaid. It would seem that the British Salt Administration office in Chungking was a product of this agreement. The British Salt Administration building survives in Chungking to this day, now situated within the grounds of a hospital on the south bank of the Yangtze river.

Brunner Mond

Brunner Mond and Company was a chemical company formed in 1873 by John Brunner and Ludwig Mond. Brunner Mond & Company became the wealthiest British chemical company of the late 19th century, with worldwide operations, including in China.

Sir John Brunner

Sir John Tomlinson Brunner (1842 – 1919) was a British chemical industrialist, Liberal Party politician and great grandfather of HRH The Duchess of Kent. He was a generous benefactor to the towns in his constituency and to the University of Liverpool. In 1873 Brunner formed a partnership with Ludwig Mond, a Jewish-born German, later naturalized British, whom he met in Widnes. Brunner Mond & Company specialised in making alkali by a new method known as the Solvay process, which produced soda ash more cheaply than the established process and produced fewer waste products. Brunner Mond brought the Solvay process to commercial viability, solving some of the problems in the process that had made mass production difficult. Within 20 years the business had become the largest producer of soda in the world.

Ludwig Mond

In 1926 Brunner Mond merged with three other British chemical companies to form Imperial Chemical Industries (ICI), an organisation that grew to become one of the world's largest and most successful companies. In 1926, ICI had a market capitalization of over £18 million (£770 million as of 2010). It reverted to the name Brunner Mond in 1991, following the sell off of the company's soda ask business. The Brunner Mond plants continue to produce sodium bicarbonate, calcium chloride and associated alkaline chemicals, and the company continues to trade in China.

The end of the treaty port era

From the 1920s onwards, the situation for foreign merchants operating in China became increasingly difficult given local political troubles, and trading levels began to decline. Foreign homes and businesses in Chungking and other treaty ports were frequently the target of violence, the banks began to collapse and foreign steamships on the Yangtze were often forced to carry troops for the different warlords, making their operations increasingly uneconomic. Several of the smaller companies were forced out of business, some selling their ships to the China Navigation Company. In this manner the latter acquired MacKenzie and Company's famous *Loong Mow* in 1923 which was renamed *Wanliu I,* and the Dollar Line's *Alice Dollar* in 1926 which was renamed *Wantung.*

Another death knell for the British presence in Chungking was a major fire in August 1924, which as usual started amongst the wooden shacks along the waterfront, then swept through the business quarter. Over one hundred people burnt to death, and many remaining foreign businesses went up in flames.

British shipping was supreme on the Upper Yangtze for the last few years of the treaty port era, since political troubles hampered Chinese shipping in these years, and anti-

Japanese boycotts led to the virtual disappearance of Japanese shipping for long periods. Not that these last few years were trouble-free for British ships. Then when Japan gained control of the Lower Yangtze at the end of 1937, the British presence on the Yangtze rapidly declined. Hankow became the capital before Nanking fell to the Japanese in December 1937, and Chungking succeeded Hankow before the latter fell in October 1938. As the Japanese moved up the river the British steamers moved ahead of them as far as possible, maintaining an increasingly restricted service, which by mid 1940 had been reduced to infrequent trips between Chungking and Wanhsien. During this period many Lower River steamers were abandoned. By mid 1940 the situation had become impossible, fuel was unobtainable, and the last few British officers were evacuated from Chungking by the new road to Kunming, then by the French railway to Haiphong, and finally by sea to Hong Kong. At this time there were two Royal Navy gunboats still at Chungking, HMS *Falcon* and *Gannet.* The former remained to act as radio link for the British Embassy, while the latter was decommissioned and her crew sent to Hong Kong by the same route.

During the heyday of the treaty port era from 1842 - 1943, foreign powers established more than 80 treaty ports on Chinese soil. Some were very successful in boosting trade;

others less so, not living up to the expectations placed on them in terms of business.

There remained throughout this period two distinct business environments in China: Shanghai and the rest of the country. In Shanghai, one could almost operate as in any foreign city: the structures were there for foreign residents to maintain a reasonably comfortable standard of living, immerse themselves as much as possible in western comforts, and conduct business reasonably easily.

Life for the British in treaty ports outside Shanghai was much more of an adventure and only the hardiest of travellers could stand it. Western China remained poor, primitive, insular and largely inaccessible, making doing business difficult.

Although British commercial shipping operations on the Yangtze and on the China coast came to an end in 1940, the official death knell came in 1943. On the 11th January of that year China concluded new treaties, on a basis of equality and reciprocity, with Britain and the United States. This ended the period of the 'Unequal Treaties' and the 'treaty port' era. Not only British shipping in Chinese waters, but significant British and Western influence in China on the former pattern, came to an end.

After the Communist revolution in 1949 it became increasingly difficult for those few remaining British companies to continue to trade. Companies still operating in China at that time included the British-American Tobacco Company, the Kailan Mining Administration – 50% British owned, and the Asiatic Petroleum Company (Shell). The main reason for the demise in the business environment was the rigid enforcement by the new Government of regulations which often ignored economic facts. There was a lack of raw materials, businesses were not allowed to dismiss staff for fear on the Government's part of mass unemployment, taxes were too high and prices for goods were often fixed below production cost rates. Failure to comply with the regulations would bring the owner of the company up against the full force of the law.

All of this had a damning effect on British trade with China and within a few years almost all British trading interests had left the country. China's appeal as a trading partner came to an abrupt pause.

But Britain left an enormous legacy in terms of trade with China. By the early 1920's British investment in the Yangtze Valley, including Shanghai, was over £200 million. This was almost as much as was invested in the whole of British India at that time, and much more than was invested in British Africa[xxi].

The East India Company was instrumental in the creation of today's system of global connections and international trade. Its activities transformed lives in Britain, Asia and beyond. It was one of the world's first multinational corporations. More specific to western China, Britain opened up the river trade on the upper Yangtze, reducing transport times through the introduction of modern machinery and navigational techniques. She also contributed greatly to the expansion of passenger trade between the treaty ports on the Upper Yangtze during the latter years of the treaty port era.

Secondly, there was a large increase in the import of products which improved the quality of everyday life for the Chinese, such as kerosene. The introduction of kerosene lamps revolutionized family life in rural areas, providing light at night and heat for cooking. Some western manufactured goods also became popular. A Times article of 1892 states that foreign cotton umbrellas were popular, *"on account of their lightness. They are displacing the clumsy native umbrellas.. and in Chengdu, they are taking the place of the large straw hats formerly in fashion"*. Then there was British tobacco. *"No trade has prospered...during the past two years more than the foreign cigarette trade ...From Tachien-lu to Mengtsz, from Chung-king to Bhamo, one is rarely out of sight of the well-known flaring posters in the Chinese characters advertising the British cigarette"*, writes Edwin

Dingle[xxii].

A number of western Chinese imports to Britain also provide invaluable. Tung oil was a valuable wood oil used in the manufacture of high quality paints and varnishes[xxiii]. Silk and tea remained as popular as ever. A fashion for Chinoiserie was huge in Britain in the 18th and 19th centuries and has had a lasting impact on western perceptions of China.

Chapter 3:

<u>Diplomacy</u>

"There is cause for apprehension lest in centuries or millennia to come China may be endangered by collision with the nations of the West"

Emperor Kang Xi, 1717

Generally speaking, most 19th century documents on British foreign policy barely give China a mention. China was insignificant in global terms. It was viewed as corrupt and backward, and only became of interest as western appetites for empire and trade began to grow. China's potential for trade attracted attention, but also generated irritation on the part of ambitious and powerful governments, such as Britain. China was viewed as doing everything it could to block western influence and hinder the establishment of trade.

British diplomatic presence in China was a product of the first opium war. As we know, the desire to establish diplomatic relations with China was driven by trade, and by far the largest part of western trade with China was British.

Diplomats from the British Consular service were sent into the interior of China as early as the 1850s to assess the commercial potential of inland China. The information they sought enabled politicians and businessmen of the day to assess whether it was worthwhile pressing on so deep into inland and western China, or better to leave the region alone. These diplomatic assessments also sought to gather information on the activities of other western powers in China's interior, particularly the French who already had a stronghold in Indo-China and saw the south-western province of Yunnan as being within its jurisdiction.

The fact that in February 1886 the British Empire had annexed Upper Burma and added it to British India must have also added impetus to entry to China as now the British Empire bordered directly on the Chinese provinces of Szechwan and Yunnan. The Yangtze River was therefore not Britain's sole access to Western China: the overland trails connecting Yunnan and Upper Burma provided new possibilities which would have increased the fact-finding missions by British diplomats. The British vision was to open up a corridor between British India and British treaty ports in China to facilitate trade.

Being a diplomatic officer in China was not an easy task. An adventurous spirit was essential, as well as the ability to endure incredible hardships as the officers toured remote parts of the country, overnighting in sub-standard accommodation, to assess the opportunities for trade, trying to engage with suspicious local officials and deal with the problems faced by the disparate British community, largely missionaries, explorers and entrepreneurs.

In the early days of Britain's diplomatic presence in China, there was little contact between Chinese and British officials at all. Chinese officials did everything in their power to distance themselves from the foreign powers they saw as invading their country. Trade was conducted through a series of "hongs", middlemen who acted as brokers and super intendents of foreign trade, largely circumventing the need for further contact at an official level. But as more and more Britons moved to China for reasons of trade, religion or simply adventure, the need for diplomatic contact increased, and was also a means of claiming access to Chinese territory in the form of treaty ports where foreigners could legally reside.

Britain was the first country to open up a diplomatic presence in western China, in Chungking, in 1877. This had been made possible by the Chefoo Agreement which extracted Chinese agreement to the stationing of a British consular agent in Chungking, but accepted a Chinese proviso that Chungking should not at that time be opened to foreign trade. The city was not in fact opened to foreign trade until 1891. Pending that, the main consular functions at Chungking were to see that the treaty provisions about transit passes were observed and by extensive travel to find out as much about western China and its resources.

Alexander Hosie was the first British Consul to Chungking, stationed there from 1882 – 1884. At this time, Chungking had not yet been reached by steamship, the Yangtze still judged unnavigable above Yichang. He was sent there chiefly to assess the potential of this remote part of the Chinese Empire for trade. He recorded his experiences in the book "Three Years in Western China: A Narrative of

Three Journeys in Szechwan, Kweichow and Yunnan', published in 1890. In his mission to assess the commercial potentiality of this remote part of China, Hosie obtained a general passport from the local authorities, hired a group of carriers and spent many months trekking around the region. He is said to have covered over 5000 miles in 3 years. He was interested not only in the passability of roads, the density of population, agricultural goods being produced in the fields, the presence of mines, but also in the variety and size of industries in western China.

There can be little doubt that Hosie played a role in focussing the attention of colonial policymakers on Chungking as an important link in the expanding network of trade. During his travels he made detailed notes and these observations were published by the Foreign Office in the form of Parliamentary Papers in 1883, 1884 and 1885. When Hosie was on home leave in late 1885 and 1886, he gave accounts of some of the most interesting parts of his findings, for example during lectures at the Royal Geographical Society and the Manchester Chamber of Commerce. The positive reaction to these lectures may have given him the idea to present his travels in Western China in a book for the general public.

As well as educating people about the prospects for trade with western China, Hosie also contributed to British scientific knowledge about Chinese agricultural practices, flora, fauna and even its tribal languages. A journey in 1884 north of Chungking focused on collecting information on Chinese insect wax for the benefit of the Royal Botanical Gardens at Kew. During his years in China, Hosie collected thousands of specimens which he sent to scientific institutions in Singapore, Hong Kong and to Kew for analysis. In honour of his contribution to knowledge an order of plants was named after him, the *ormosia hossiei*. An Annex to his book contains a short study on the language of the Miao of Guizhou, or the "Pho" as he refers to them.

The Opening of Chungking to foreign trade, and the arrival of steam travel to and from the city, meant that by 1897, the Consul was needed in his office daily and was no longer free to travel as extensively in the surrounding region of over half a million square miles which came under his consular jurisdiction. That year Litton, a brash Irish Etonian was selected and sent to Chungking to act as Consular assistant at the British Consulate to enable the Consul to renew his travels. The choice proved a bad one. Litton was young, had negligible experience and a hothead. His superiors in Peking classed his reports as *"wild, alarming and sent by a man who had lost his head"*. Litton was reprimanded and asked to leave the city.

Chungking was a diplomatic posting for the hardy and did not inspire consular affection. In 1905 Campbell described it as the most disagreeable Chinese city he had ever visited, *"a dripping, mouldy, crass ant-heap where everything was damp and draggled."*[xxiv]

It was difficult to reach, once there life was comfortless, and there was appreciable risk. The journey by junk to Chungking was hazardous. Getting a junk through the rapids, whirlpools and against the current required great skill and haulage by trackers. Fatal accidents were frequent, and the time taken for the journey was unpredictable. In 1881, it took Spence 58 days from Ichang to Chungking. He was held up by floods, once for twelve days and once for seven days, two men were drowned when a junk in company with him was in a collision, the steersman of his own junk was washed overboard in a whirlpool and drowned, and when safer water was reached two sweeps broke, tow ropes broke repeatedly, and finally the junk hit a rock and sank, luckily in shallow water.[xxv]

As well as prospecting for trade, the job of the Consuls was to look after the interests of British nationals living in the region and to intervene where necessary with the Chinese authorities to uphold British rights under the treaties. When attacks against foreigners occurred, there were set procedures to follow for foreigners to register a complaint with the authorities, backed up by the resident Consul. Technically the local Mandarin was held responsible for the attack and could be degraded. But in practice, the position of the local magistrates meant to enforce this procedure was difficult, caught between instructions from Peking to protect foreigners and strong local anti-foreigner feeling.

The Consul therefore often found himself in a difficult position: trying to defence Britain's rights under the treaties, but often being thwarted from doing so. The Consul's position was made more difficult given they were often operating in small remote communities where foreign communities consisted mainly of small numbers of businessman and a majority of missionaries – the latter often considered by their own government as troublemakers. The large numbers of missionaries, particularly Roman Catholics, in western China led to increased suspicion of foreigners more generally.

After long years of service as a Consul in China, Alcock said that he considered treaty port society about as bad as it could be, with little public opinion and a very low moral tone... Culture and even education were in short supply.[xxvi]. Most residents would refuse to learn any Chinese, they were young, mainly male and looking for adventure, and violence and intemperance were marked features of treaty port life.

In order to get their job done then, Consuls had to be discreet when travelling around the countryside, always doing so in an official chair and not drawing too much attention to themselves. Baber, Consul to Chungking in the late 1870s wrote that *"no traveller in Western China who possesses any sense of self-respect should journey without a sedan chair, not necessarily as a conveyance, but for the honour and glory of the thing. Unfurnished with this indispensable token of respectability he is liable to be thrust aside on the highway, to be kept waiting at ferries, to be relegated to the worst inn's worst room, and generally to be treated with indignity, or, what is sometimes worse, with familiarity, as a peddling footpad who, unable to gain a living in his own country, has come to subsist on China."*[xxvii]

Some, such as Parker, who served in Chungking some years later was less discreet, putting himself in much danger. He liked to walk out in the streets twice daily for exercise. This resulted in rumours that the Englishman had killed a child or had caused a drought by an act of impiety. A threatening mob of some 2000 people gathered outside his house and crept into the gate with a coffin. In trying to escape over the garden wall, he fell off and sprained both ankles. The magistrate, to whom he had sent, arrived in time to save him, but Parker was understandably shaken. A doctor assessed that Parker had been very severely affected morally by the incident, and the Foreign Office ordered him to go on home leave to recover.

In another incident in 1886, Consul Bourne met a riot in which, with one exception, every foreign residence in the city was looted or destroyed, as were the houses of converts. Gardner at Hankow forwarded to the Legation in Peking a despatch he received from Bourne. It was written on two small pieces of paper in a firm and rapid hand and was sent from the Chungking intendent's yamen, where Bourne had taken refuge. Hearing of a riot against the China Inland Mission members Bourne had gone to the yamen to ask for protection, and for his return journey was escorted by a guard of forty men under an officer. The guard were no match for the mob that confronted them. Bourne's chair was smashed with huge stones which hurt him badly on an arm and a leg, a stick hit him on the temple, and for half an hour he expected to be murdered at any minute. His clear and matter of fact despatch ended, *"The affair looks now as bad as it can be and I am doubtful whether I shall ever write another letter".*

His retrospective opinion was that foreigners had escaped with their lives only because the Margary affair had shown how expensive and troublesome it was to murder them, and that had he remained in his house he would have been murdered, for being ignorant of the extent of the riot he would probably have shot some of the first comers.

In the first two decades after opening the only British Consul to last more than a couple of years was J.N. Tratman, who occupied the post between 1894 and 1898. Tratman's stint took a heavy toll on his health and nerves. After a long medical furlough he returned to the China service a broken, indifferent time-server, and had to take early retirement[xxviii].

When not travelling around the region prospecting for trade, the life of the Consul revolved around forming good relations with local officials in order to solve disputes and uphold British rights under the Treaties.

Business with Chinese officials was conducted by interviews and written communications, both time-consuming. The journey by chair to and from an interview might be wearisomely lengthy, and fraught with danger. All correspondence had to be translated. Most Consuls were competent in the written language and did not need a translation to comprehend inward communications, but translations had to be made for the consulate archives, so that the Foreign Office in London had a hold on what was going on in-country.

Relations with Chinese officials tended to be courteous at most, but nothing more. Chinese officials would have risked their social reputations and their careers by being on noticeably friendly personal terms with a foreigner. Many officials were found unfriendly, ignorant and obstructive. Some were merely ridiculous: a Shanghai magistrate attributed his predecessor's death to the malign geomantic influence of the steeple of an American missionary church. His fear of similar buildings and their effect on his life expectancy led him to arrest Chinese who had sold land near his yamen to British missionaries, thereby causing a diplomatic incident.

A Consul who failed to obtain satisfaction by badgering the local authorities at interviews and bombarding them with despatches and letters had reached the end of normal procedures. In theory the dispute could then be referred to the chief superintendent and raised by him with his opposite number.

Some Consuls considered it more effective to take matters into their own hands and direct British subjects to stop paying customs duties locally until redress was obtained. It also proved effective to threaten to call in the British navy as a form of consular pressure.

From the early 1900s, when interest in the West began to grow, diplomatic relations became slightly more cordial. The concept of doing business over food then became more part of the diplomatic environment, as it is today. It was here, around a table of food and drink, that relationships were formed to allow diplomatic business to be done. Descriptions of such dinners do not differ much from the type of affair that I had to endure as a diplomat in Chongqing. Archibald Little records one dinner thrown in his honour in comic detail worth recording in full here:

"Then, in my honour, followed the usual Chinese dinner-party, which to the Western is an intolerably tedious affair. Seven of us sat down to a small square table; I, as the guest of the day, having a seat at the top all to myself, the others sitting two each on short benches. The table was adorned at starting with sixteen large set dishes of highly flavoured mincemeats, fruits, and vegetables, and about a dozen saucers containing melon seeds, peanuts, candied orange peel &c – the centre being occupied by the "removes", which are replaced successively a dozen times or more throughout the feast, and consist chiefly of fat pork cooked in various ways. The business of the day commenced with swallowing endless thimblefuls of hot "sam-shu", a fiery spirit made from millet; interspersed with the cracking of melon seeds and pea-nuts, and the tasting of the different dishes with chop-

sticks; the Lilliputian saucer in front of the honoured guests being heaped up with tit-bits, fished out with the chop-sticks of the too polite hosts.

Gradually, after all have drunk well, the removes are seriously attacked, when the company after about two hours' time, being absolutely unable to swallow any more food, wine-drinking recommences, stimulated by the noisy, and to the Chinaman highly exciting game of Morra, in which I am fairly proficient. All this time, not a morsel of bread or grain of rice to assist the deglutition of the greasy dishes, only occasional hot cloths to wipe the mouth, and the perspiring brow, and a few whiffs of the common hubble-bubble which a lad is told off to constantly hand round to each guest. This he does, the burning match in one hand, the pipe in the other, presenting the long brass stem to the mouth. Little red paper napkins, five inches by two, are folded before each guest, but are totally inefficient to wipe away the grease spots, with which the varnished table at an early period gets covered; bones, gristle, &c., being spat out on the floor to mingle with the tobacco from the perpetually relighted pipes. All the while, one is seated on a high, hard, wooden stool, which is torture to a weary Western traveller, but on which the Chinese loll about from morning to night".

He goes on to describe how only when the oily main dishes have been finished is rice then served, and the bowl, if accepted, must be emptied to the last grain, or else the guest is judged as totally wanting in manners. I can well imagine the frustration and bemused comedy of the situation Little must have felt to have rushed home and felt the need to commit a detailed description of the *"tediousness and absence of all real comfort"* of the Chinese formal dinner experience to paper.[xxix]

Notes from Consuls to Chungking over the years are enough to give a picture of the difficult conditions they had to endure.

Initially there was a complete lack of company or recreation. Parker, who served in western China in the 1880s, said in 1881 that in nine months he had in all spent at most twenty-four hours in European company. Coming towards the end of nearly four years in Chungking in 1890, Cockburn spoke of an unspeakably dreary life of solitude in a most depressing climate. In 1898 Litton, in only his second year at Chungking, began applying for home leave or for a transfer away from a post which in his opinion was one of the East's most depressing stations. He complained that the existing consulate was a dark, dilapidated Chinese house in the filthiest quarter of one of China's filthiest towns, that it had for neighbours coolies, pedlars, and women of the lowest class, and that a new consulate could have been built for half the amount paid in exorbitant rents.[xxx]

Captain William Gill visiting Chungking in 1870s was little impressed with the official residence of British consular representative, Edward Baber, finding it unfitting for such a global power:

An entrance with folding doors leads into a second court 25 feet by 20 broad. The first half is covered with a roof of tiles and on each side are rooms divided from the court by wooden partitions, the upper half of which is open trellis work (this in winter is covered with paper) opposite the entrance. Three steps lead into the main room 14 feet by 17 feet and 12 feet high. The floor is of stone and mud, the walls of wood, that on the side towards the court does not come to within three inches of the ground and the upper half is open trellis work. On each side of the main room is a bedroom, each of these the same size as the sitting room but with no entrance for light except the door and a little hole in the roof.

On each side of the sitting room are four stiff uncompromising armchairs with a good deal of carving of dragons and between each chair is a little high square table. These are stained like old mahogany and polished.

Imagine the walls and roof to be about as dirty as they well can be and you may have some idea of the house Her Majesty's representative occupies at Ch'ung Ch'ing [Chongqing]."

In 1913, WR Brown wrote from the consulate that without exception every officer stationed there had made every effort to escape as soon as possible; the permanent winter cloud filled the most sanguine with despair; the blazing summer sun drew out each smell from incredibly filthy streets and blended it into one indescribable whole; outside society and amusement were unobtainable; and only an officer with inward resources could hope to remain there without mental impairment. In 1881 Consular agent Parker wrote that in nine months he had in all spent at most twenty-four hours in European company. Litton, in only his second year at Chongqing in 1898, began applying for home leave or for a transfer away from a post which in his opinion was one of the East's most depressing stations[xxxi]

Supplies which foreigners considered necessities could not be bought locally. In 1882 the tinned and bottled stores which Spence took with him for a short stay in Chungking included jam, marmalade, butter, coffee beans, baking and curry powder, two casks of Apollinaris water, and nine dozen bottles of wine and spirits, and the Legation certified that the cost of shipment was a perfectly reasonable expense. Medical attention, the greatest need, was a month's journey away in 1887. But in 1892 the Treasury, assured that in parts of China the climate was unusually healthy and invigorating, jibbed at designating Chungking an unhealthy post for pension purposes unless they were given direct evidence that Chungking's climate was exceptionally injurious to men of ordinarily vigorous constitution. They were persuaded to give way….[xxxii].

Into the 20th century there were continued complaints about the accommodation provided for diplomats, and the long commute many had to endure, by chair and across the Yangtze in a sampan, from their homes in the foreign area on the south bank of the Yangtze to the Consulate building in the city centre – often as much as a two hour journey each way.

Other treaty ports in south-west China

As the British government's knowledge of western China increased, so did its ambitions to open up further strategically-placed towns and cities to trade. In total six treaty ports were eventually opened by the British in western China: Chungking, Chengtu, Tachienlu in the foothills of Tibet, and 3 in the province of Yunnan – in Yunnanfu (present day Kunming), Tengyueh and Ssumao (present day Simao) to monitor French incursions into the province.

Chengtu was an important city in Szechwan province and had a similar-sized British population of missionaries and a few random businessmen to Chungking. Ssumao and Tengyueh were opened in the last years of the 19th century.

The Tengyueh consulate was the result of an Anglo-Chinese convention of 1894 about Burma. It acted both act as a listening post to keep an eye on French activities in nearby Indo-China, to facilitate a primitive trade between Burma and China carried by caravans of pack animals and to help settle disputes along a border both sides of which were inhabited by tribes including the peaceful Shan, the less peaceful Kachin and the head-hunting Wa. In view of these functions the Indian government met half the cost of maintaining the consulate. At this time, Tengyueh had only 1400 inhabitants and was a primitive place located in mountains 5400 feet above sea level. Consul Jamieson who arrived there in 1899 first occupied a tumbledown granary complete with leaking roof, lacking any doors and with only a nearby field as a latrine.

In the four months he was stationed in Tengyueh Jamieson acquired a reputation as a no-nonsense, straight talker, often coming into conflict with British officials in nearby Burma. But he claimed to have won the respect of local officials with his hard-talking manner and was able to walk the streets without an escort and without insult or cries of "kill the foreign devil". He also managed to get local officials to show some energy in dealing with Burmese consular cases[xxxiii].

An 1895 Sino-French convention provided for the opening of Ssumao as a treaty port to serve the trade between Yunnan and Laos in Indo-China. The journey there was a tedious one, involving four different boats from the bay of Halong, a mule caravan and a chair, taking 7 weeks in total. On arrival there, the same Jamieson mentioned above realised that the opening of a British consulate in such a remote backwater was a complete waste of money as no British trader was ever likely to go there. It was also extremely inconvenient as a place: a Hong Kong cheque could not be sold there so silver ingots had to be transported which were cumbersome and provided for a risky journey in these dangerous parts.

Jamieson urged that the consulate be transferred from Ssumao to Yunnanfu, the provincial capital where all caravan routes through the province converged. Politically a consulate there would show the French that Britain did not mean to be shut out of that part of Yunnan and would stiffen the Chinese against the French. Britain needed to strengthen her position in this province bordering Szechwan, which in any partition of China by western powers, it was hoped should be included within the British sphere of influence.

The hot-headed Litton, who was earlier dismissed from his post in Chungking, was the strange choice to replace Jamieson in Ssumao. His opinion of Ssumao was little better than Jamieson's: in a trade report of rather pungent language, which required considerable editing before the Foreign Secretary was given it to read, he classed Ssumao as no more than a village, its communications were execrable, there was no evidence of conditions being suitable for the flourishing of commerce and that as a political listening post it was equally useless.

Litton's presence in Ssumao lasted all of three months. Shortly before he left he was attacked by Wa tribesmen wielding stones and knocked unconscious. When he came to, he shot one of his aggressors, causing the others to back off. Litton seems to have gone on home leave soon after this incident and after him no member of the consular service was stationed at Ssumao.

Tachienlu was another strange choice for a consulate, opened in 1913. Situated 10,000 feet above sea level in Szechwan's mountainous and ethnically Tibetan marches, it was a full 12 days' journey over punishing terrain from Chengtu. Its purpose was predominantly political – to report on Chinese troop movements in the region and report them back to British India along with their potential impact on Tibet's status, then seen as an important buffer state between the Chinese and Russian empires and British India. On arrival at Tachienlu, Consul L. M King reported that it contained a resident population of 1600 families, half ethnically Chinese and half Tibetan, and a floating population of some 5000 tea coolies and yak drivers. Everything the consul needed had to be transported to Tachienlu, including food, as little could be procured along the way. On his first journey there, King was accompanied by a writer, 3 personal servants, 2 interpreters, 5 pony drivers, 22 yaks and 24 porters.

King lived in barn-like quarters which were meagrely furnished and full of icicles. The surrounding countryside was too mountainous for walking or riding, and the only other recreational activity available was social contact with a semi-insane frontier commissioner, with whom King became good friends. King ended up returning to Tachienlu twice on separate postings and even bore a child with a local Tibetan woman, whom he eventually took back to England and married.

Such was its political importance that the British mission in Tachienlu remained opened until 1922, when it was decided that the mission in Chengtu would takeover the duties of Tachienlu. Unfortunately Tachienlu's very interesting archives were lost to bandits in a raid on the former consulate in 1924 so many of its stories have been lost to history[xxxiv].

The end of the treaty port era

Into the 1920s there was increasing violence in western China from the activities of local warlords. Some of this was directed towards foreign residents. Diplomatic officers played an important role in ensuring the security of foreign residents in the area, regularly issuing instructions to them to vacate their homes and take refuge on British naval vessels anchored on the Yangtze for their protection, or ordering evacuation of the city altogether.

During a particularly bad incident in 1924, as Chungking was plastered with anti-British slogans, the Consul took refuge on the gunboat while the other foreigners took refuge in the foreign godowns on the south bank of the Yangtze near

Lungmenhao. As the incident got worse, sailors were landed from the gunboat to protect the foreigners on land. The crowd stoned and rushed at them causing panic and leading three men to be wounded by bayonets. Some foreigners, including all the women and children, finally managed to escape by steamer, but 27 others were besieged by a cordon of Chinese boy scouts aiming to starve them out. The incident eventually dissipated, but not until all the foreign bungalows on the hills had been looted and smashed up.

Another role of the Consul was to organise and host incoming visits by visiting British dignitaries. These would have been few and far between in this remote corner of China but in 1926, Chungking was graced with the visit of British royalty, in the form of young Prince George, later Duke of Kent, who was came to visit the Yangtze flotilla and offer his support and gratitude for the efforts of the Royal Navy in protecting British interests in western China. Price George was taken to visit the Quakers' Boys High School where the American community were holding their annual 4th of July celebrations. A few days later he was there again, for a tea party given in his honour by the British Chamber of Commerce[xxxv].

Throughout the late 1920s and early 1930s the British population of Chungking began to dwindle against the growing backdrop of violence and decline. But Chungking once again became a focus of international attention during the Second World War as the wartime capital of China. The city's population grew fast as Chinese factories, universities and officials flooded into the city. Chungking also saw an influx of foreigners during this period, including missionaries eager to help China's war effort and care for the injured; foreign correspondents covering the war; an increase in foreign diplomats to work at newly relocated embassies; and foreign servicemen brought in to assist China's war effort and protect foreign interests in the city.

The British Consulate in Linshi Xiang was upgraded to an Embassy. Diplomats stationed in the city during the Second World War played a vital role in reporting back what was happening on the ground in western China and the damage the Japanese were inflicting on the Chinese wartime capital, but it was a dangerous time. The British Embassy, in the centre of the city, was repeatedly bombed. The Times reported on 29 June 1940 that the offices of the British diplomatic mission and Consulate-General were made completely uninhabitable and the operating and x-ray rooms of the American Methodist hospital demolished during an air raid. Mr Broadmead, the Acting Counsellor, and the Assistant Military Attache, Major Millar, who were both in the Embassy's dugout, were badly shaken by the blast but not hurt. The following summer, a heavy bomb fell on the lower part of the Embassy compound severely damaging the new Press Attache's office, and the blast from bombs falling on adjoining buildings damaged the main offices of the Embassy. No one was hurt[xxxvi].

British Ambassador to China Sir Archibald Kerr moved permanently from Peking to Chungking in 1940. He resided high up on the highest mountain in the city, high above the south bank of the Yangtze, in a Chinese –style house built by admirers of Chiang Kai Shek for his family, but rented by Chiang Kai Shek to the British Ambassador. This building still exists today, hidden in the forests that cover the mountainside above modern-day Chongqing and difficult to access. British resident Robert Payne describes a visit to the Ambassador's house as follows:

"Once inside the Ambassador's house, we were in another world. In a small room, which was once the pavilion of a Chinese general, a great log fire was blazing. There were photographs, enormous bookcases, a collie dog, and comfortable armchairs – a sense of security and good taste, of quiet contemplation and infinite common sense... Sir Archibald Kerr came in five minutes later. He had been walking along the cliffs, and he brought with him the tang of winter on the Scottish moors. He wore a check coat and grey flannel trousers; the long aquiline nose, the sunburn and the bushy eyebrows were those of a Scottish laird, and his

enormous hands were like the hands of an artist.... We waited. A clock was ticking sonorously on the mantelpiece – an English clock, even to the little whirring sound before the chimes. And once more he returned, and the room was flooded with the scent of heather and pines, and on our imagination we were travelling through some distant landscape of Scotland, where the mist was the same as the mist of Chungking and even the sampans and the people in the crowded streets were the same."xxxvii

Robert Payne, a British expat who came to China to teach English literature at the refugee Chinese National University just outside Chongqing, describes conditions in Chungking at that time in his book "Chungking Diary". Of a typical air raid he says:

"Late in the evening there was an air alarm; the red triangles were hoisted on the mast above the Meifung Bank, and the Street of the Seven Stars was in swirling flood – people were rushing in every direction, small carts piled with luggage, rickshas weighed down with six or seven packing cases, even bicycles were loaded with the family property. The shutters went down with a bang. Motor cars – too many motorcars – went screaming into the countryside. There is something merciless in this great river of people rushing down the streets in the dust and smoke of the evening, something terrifying, resembling the Yangtze in full flood.

They run, not because they are afraid, but because the sound of the sirens and the great triangles on the high buildings remind them of the past; and instinctively they race towards the shelters. Even if they took no thought of running, their limbs would carry them away...

Then the aeroplanes came. They swung down very low over the city, the sound of the roaring engines echoing in the deserted streets. Light night hawks, their wings glittering in the moonlight. I do not know why but I was not afraid. I remembered a story I had read many years ago of a man walking through a bombarded city, not mad, but entirely alone and detached from the world.... A British subject in China has, or should have, the right to call upon the Ambassador at moments of great crisis. I wandered along to the British Embassy, where there were dugouts, though rumour had it that the previous Ambassador had never used them".

During this period Chungking is thought to have been the most heavily bombed city in history. From February 1938 to August 1943 more than 5000 Japanese Imperial Air Force bombing runs with over 11,500 bombs dropped on the city's mostly civilian population[xxxviii].

On 11 January 1943 in wartime Chungking the British Ambassador signed a Sino-British treaty abolishing extraterritoriality and returning the remaining concessions and foreign settlements to China. Simultaneously in Washington, a Sino-American treaty with the same stipulations was signed by the Chinese Ambassador and the US secretary of State. This effectively brought an end to the treaty port era

By the end of the war in 1946, the damage to the city of Chungking was extensive. Over 3000 tons of bombs were dropped on the city during the Second World War as a whole, in 268 different air raids. At the end of the war, the Chinese transferred the capital city first to Nanjing, and then following the revolution in 1949 back to Beijing. This also marked the end of Britain, and other countries' diplomatic presence in western China for several decades.

By 1951 the doors finally closed on the British Consulate in Chungking and a period of history came to an end. Foreign residents left China in their droves as their homes in protected settlements ceased to exist. With the arrival of the Communists to power in 1949, business also became near impossible. By 1950 the British Chamber of Commerce in Shanghai acknowledged that it was all over: not only were firms facing bankruptcy, but the lack of regulation made it dangerous even to attempt transactions.

On 6 January 1950 the British government recognized the People's Republic of China as the legitimate government of

China – the first major western country to do so - and posted a chargé d'affaires *ad interim* in Beijing. The British expected a rapid exchange of Ambassadors, but this did not happen as the PRC demanded concessions on the Chinese seat at the UN and the foreign assets of the Republic of China, which Britain was unable to grant.

A Foreign Office report on the situation in China for British nationals in 1951 speaks of *"a distressing story of the progressive decline of our once flourishing interests in China"*. The numbers of Britons in the country as a whole was estimated to have fallen from 20,000 in 1937 to 5000 in 1945 and just 1700 in 1951. UK-China relations were finally upgraded to full Ambassadorial level in 1972 when Britain withdraw its support for Taiwan to occupy China's seat at the UN.

From the 1950s to the 1980s, during the turbulent years of the Great Leap Forward and Cultural Revolution most foreigners left China, and China once again closed its doors to the outside world.

Deng Xiaoping initiated another period of "reform and opening up" from 1979. Intrepid British businessmen began to slowly return and Britain's diplomatic presence in Beijing began to grow again. A number of trade missions were led to western China during this period to prospect for new trade opportunities. Given the move of many strategic industries to Chungking during the Second World War, Chungking had become an important industrial centre in the intervening years, including a major centre for automotive production and Asia's biggest producer of motorbikes.

The real turning point came in the year 2000 when, almost 50 years after it had closed, Britain decided to reopen a Consulate-General in Chongqing to take full advantage of trade opportunities in the region. And that is how I came to be in Chongqing – possibly the world's fastest growing city – at the start of the 21st century.

Legacy of the Consuls

So what was the legacy of all these Foreign Office men and women who dedicated years of their live to reporting from and serving the British community in this far-flung corner of western China?

They contributed to keeping thousands of Britons safe during this turbulent period of Chinese history. They negotiated the treaties which allowed greater British and foreign access to the Chinese market, ultimately contributing to further trade and opening up new commercial opportunities for Britain in the west of China. Their writings provide historic evidence of conditions in the country at that time.

But more than that, the earlier Consuls in particular displayed great acts of courage and adventure, often against incredible adversity and hostility, in furthering knowledge about the region. Alexander Hosie contributed greatly to the study of botany. During his many years in China he collected and sent thousands of specimens to scientific institutions in Singapore, Hong Kong and to Kew Gardens in London. In honour of his contribution to knowledge an order of plants was named after him, the Ormosia hosiei.

Baber received the coveted Gold Medal of the Royal Geographical Society for his contribution to knowledge about western China. In his personal records Baber describes the misery of mapping the day's journey by flickering rush light in a single room without doors and windows, huddled in dripping clothes amid blinding smoke over a brushwood fire and fortified only by a meal of potatoes and maize, but he was the fortunate possessor of a keen sense of humour. He had the inspired notion of travelling with a pet monkey, whose peculiarity diverted popular attention from his own lesser peculiarity, and he took in his stride the theft of all his money while he slept in the wilds[xxxix].

Joseph Needham, science Counsellor at the British Embassy in Chungking from 1942-1946, is perhaps the best known of Britain's diplomats to have served in Chungking. He went on to found what became the British Council in

China and write the longest book in the English language about China – still much admired today. His contribution to science and furthering knowledge about China's achievements in this area, is covered in full in Chapter 6.

Previous pages:

- Chongqing street seller, 2010
- Treaty port era building, central Chongqing
- Old districts of central Chongqing earmarked for demolition, 2010
- Treaty port era building earmarked for demolition, 2010
- Former Canadian consulate, Chongqing
- Former Canadian consulate, Chongqing
- Former Canadian consulate, Chongqing
- View of central peninsula of Chongqing from Nanshan mountain

Chapter 4:

<u>Lifestyle and culture</u>

"China generally is not at all like the willow-pattern plate. I do not know if I really expected it to be blue and white; but it was a disappointment to find it so very brown and muddy."

Alicia Little, Intimate China: The Chinese as I have seen them (1899)"[xl]

Foreign residents in Chungking in the late 19th and early 20th centuries found themselves in a world which contrasted sharply with their own. This was not even the China that some of them had experienced on the eastern seaboard – with its foreign concessions of fine European houses, public parks, wide streets with electric lights, dancehalls and restaurants. This was particularly true of Shanghai – many Europeans' first glimpse of China – where *"everything that could possibly be wanted could be bought and only very little dearer than in London"*[xli]

Chungking was raw China: a mountainous city, deep in China's interior which had had previous little contact with the outside world. It lay behind the formidable Three Gorges of the Yangtze with its wild currents, eddies and hidden rocks, through which ships had to be hauled by teams of trackers, making it inaccessible and an Eldorado for the more intrepid traveller.

In historic documents Chongqing has been likened to Quebec – given its situation at the confluence of two great rivers; to Edinburgh – due to its hilly topography; to Lyon – similar in size; and nicknamed *"the Liverpool of western China"*, given its prominent role as a commercial centre and important port.

These descriptions make the city sound vaguely familiar, akin to something travellers of the time would know or be able to relate to. But those early foreign residents and visitors who made the treacherous journey through the Three Gorges were totally unprepared for what they found in Chungking, reflected in the numerous vivid descriptions of the place found in their diaries and papers.

The Chongqing of yesteryear must have been a formidable sight. Situated on a narrow rocky peninsula between the Yangtze and Jialing rivers, the city towered above the turbid waters below, the seasonal variations of which changed by some 90 feet between summer and winter. It was confined between 18th century walls with seventeen gates, sixteen of which led down to the waterfront and all but one of these gates was closed every evening to keep the fortress city safe from marauders.

The narrow neck of the promontory which afforded the only access to the city by land was covered with grave mounds, preventing the city from expanding in any direction. This was a common feature of many cities of eastern Sichuan at the time, where the dead seemed to occupy more space than the living.

Old stone steps of Chaotianmen rising from the Yangtze riverbank to the old city

Given the city's unusual topography, everything was cramped and irregular. Everywhere were long flights of steps, and given the limited possibilities for wheeled transport in such conditions, everything had to be carried on wooden carrying poles. Porters or "bang bang" men, who scrape together a living carrying goods with the aid of a length of bamboo and a rope, remain a very much a typical feature of Chongqing today, little seen in any other Chinese city. s space was limited, residents occupied any space on the peninsula they could. The Yangtze foreshore was a seasonal home to the poorest, occupying makeshift bamboo and matted housing tied together with bamboo rope in winter, and retreating back to the city in the high-water summer months. Above these were permanent wooden buildings with tiled roofs, flooded only in years of highest water. And the edge of the water was lined with houseboats, which are free to rise and fall with the river.

The Chungking of yesteryear has been immortalised in "On a Chinese Screen", a collection of short stories written by Somerset Maugham during a 1500-mile trip along the Yangtze river he undertook in the winter of 1919-1920. His depictions of the Chongqing are uncannily reminiscent of the city today:

"a grey and gloomy city, shrouded in mist, for it stands upon its rock where two great rivers meet so that it is washed on all sides but one by turbid rushing waters. The rock is like the prow of an ancient galley and seems, as though possessed of a strange, unnatural life, all tremulous with effort…

Outside the walls bedraggled houses are built on piles, and here, when the river is low, a hazardous population lives on the needs of the watermen; for at the foot of the rock a thousand junks are moored, wedged in with one another tightly, and men's lives there have all the turbulence of the river. A steep and torturous stairway leads to the great gate guarded by a temple, and up and down this all day long go the water coolies, with their dripping buckets; and from their splashing the stair and the street that leads from the gate are wet as though after heavy rain. It is difficult to walk on the level for more than a few minutes, and there are as many steps as in the hill towns of the Italian Riviera.

Because there is so little space the streets are pressed together, narrow and dark, and they wind continuously so that to find your way is like finding it in a labyrinth. The throng is as thick as the throng on a pavement in London when a theatre is emptying itself of its audience. You have to push your way through it, stepping aside every moment as chairs come by and coolies bearing their everlasting loads; itinerant sellers, selling almost anything that anyone can want to buy, jostle you as you pass."[xlii]

But the city also possessed at that time wonderful public parks and streets of fine "hongs", homes of rich local merchants, accessed through a series of courtyards. The parks were filled with pavilions of different sizes where locals could entertain guests in privacy, akin to the west's modern day private clubs. They were owned in shares by groups of friendly families who would inhabit them for an afternoon or evening complete with their own cook and provisions. These parks were located in the upper part of the city with fine views out to both sides of the peninsula.

Archibald Little describes how the city was a perfect harmony between man and nature, a place where *feng shui* in its best sense reigned supreme, and all the buildings were in keeping with the environment: "there is no sign of that strife with nature which our bold Western methods encourage. No braggart upstart building towers rudely above its neighbours, stealing their air and light. The temples and Yamens are the only buildings more conspicuous than the mass"[xliii]

Anyone who knows Chongqing today will marvel at these descriptions. Today a city of 9 million, it is considered to be one of the fastest growing cities in the world, where every day approximately 1300 rural migrants are added to its population. It is a grey city with a lack of green, open spaces, and where skyscrapers are packed in like sardines, each jostling to thrust higher into the sky than the last. Nowhere more than in Chongqing have I felt that the balance between man and nature had been so completely lost. And the fine "hongs" of the past – bar the few mentioned in this book – have been largely victims to the extensive Second World War bombing of the city or the developers' bulldozers.

The Chongqing of today remains a resolutely Chinese city: China at its best and worst. Now, as then, what first strikes foreigners about Chongqing is the smell, the noise, the crowds, the intense heat and the perpetual fog. Missionary Robert Davidson writes in the early 1900s:

"Then there were the smells. The Westerner found most Chinese cities pungent, but the stench of Chungking seems to have struck the most hardened traveller with horror. It is a charnel house smell, suggestive of mawkish disease, of rottenness of bones. It is no mere compound of open drains and the reek of perspiring men, streaked by the odour of cooking oil, incense and putrid fish. It is an aggressive smell…. As horrible in its suggestion of suffocation as if invisible fingers were clutching at the throat." In summer rats play around one's feet like spaniels and everywhere there were scavenging dogs, eleven out of ten in an advanced state of disease"[xliv].

Somerset Maugham describes *"a stench which time and experience enable you to distinguish into a thousand separate stenches. Your nostrils grow cunning. Foul odours beat upon your harassed nerves like the sound of uncouth instruments playing a horrible symphony".*[xlv]

Chongqing has one of the most miserable climates in China. Hemmed in by mountains and standing at the confluence of two big rivers, the city is humid, windless and incredibly foggy. In summer temperatures sore to over 40 degrees and, given the humidity, the result is like permanently living in a sauna. Winters are mild, but the lingering humidity, lack of heating in buildings and draughts, make it feel much colder than it really is. And visibility is often reduced to near zero for months at a time as the winter fog descends. As Somerset Maugham put it: *"They say of [Chungking] that the dogs bark when peradventure the sun shines there."*[xlvi] Coming towards the end of nearly four years in the city, British Consular agent, Cockburn in 1890 spoke of *"an unspeakably dreary life of solitude in a most depressing climate."*[xlvii] It was clear that only the most hardy of travellers could survive the isolation and hardships of expatriation in a place like Chongqing.

Alicia Little

Alicia Little has done more than anyone to describe the China, and more particularly Chongqing, of the late 19th and early 20th century from the perspective of its foreign residents.

Wife of British merchant, explorer and inventor Archibald Little, the Littles were the first foreigners to settle permanently in Chongqing in 1883. Archibald Little had first gone to China in 1857 as a tea taster for a German company.

He later set up his own trading company in Chongqing, but his real obsession was in exploring prospects for steam navigation through the Three Gorges – until that time only navigable by junk, pulled through the Gorges by trackers. He eventually became the first person to navigate a steamship through the Three Gorges in 1898.

Archibald and Alicia Little

Alicia Little was not a typical Victorian wife. She was born in Madeira in 1845 to rich British parents. She travelled widely in her youth and moved back to Britain in her early 20s to enter the debutante social circuit appropriate to acquiring a suitable husband.

But it seems Alicia was too spirited to stand the customary entertainments and preoccupations of the social season and took to writing down her sharp observations of the world she found herself in and its foibles. She published her first novel at the age of 23 called Flirts and Flirts or A Season in Ryde under her maiden name of Alicia Bewicke. Following her marriage to Archibald Little, who she described as an "innocent dreamer", full of weird and wonderful ideas and schemes, they began a new life in China.

Not content with the closeted life of a trailing spouse, Alicia was determined to engage with the Chinese society around her, rather than hide herself away at home. She made great efforts in particular to get to know the women of Chongqing. She learnt to speak fluent Chongqing dialect to communicate with them, taught English, tried to understand Chinese traditions and customs, and taught herself photography to record her experiences. She became one of the first European writers to document the lives of Chinese women and was to become one of the best-known authors writing on China around the turn of the century.

As well as novels, she wrote frequently about China for British publications of her time, putting across Chinese standpoints and providing explanations for the Chinese government's actions at a time when there was little western understanding of China. Her books about China, such as "Intimate China: The Chinese as I have seen them" and "Blue Gown" are still used by British university students of Chinese today, in their studies of Chinese society and civilisation. Her shrewd and amusing comments about Chinese society paint a very vivid description of the Chongqing of her time.

Initially foreigners were not allowed to reside in the central city of Chungking – the promontory between the rivers. They were confined to the south bank of the Yangtze river, across from the main city, and travelled by sampan across the treacherous Yangtze to do business in the main city or meet with government officials.

The Littles settled on the south bank of the Yangtze where their house remains to this day, albeit it in an advanced state of dilapidation: a highlight of European-influenced architecture in Chongqing, with its wide verandas, grand staircase, stuccoed ceilings and interesting mix of Chinese and European architectural styles. The Littles' residence was later joined on the waterfront by a number of other trading companies including Butterfield and Swires, the British Salt Administration, Brunner Mond (later known as ICI) and Standard Oil; foreign diplomatic missions and the navies of several countries, including US and British gunboats.

Pictures of the time show a rather neat looking waterfront of European-style buildings, in sharp contrast to the dishevelled Chinese city opposite. Only a scattering of these buildings still exist today.

Initially, there was a complete lack of company or recreation for the city's foreign residents. Alicia Little described the sheer sense of isolation in a place like Chungking where it took at best 4 months to receive a letter from England, and that the distance somehow seemed to deter people from writing even more! As she put it, *"the result tends to heighten the sense of isolation, which is perhaps nowhere so much felt as among the Chinese. Whether it is their expressionless, their want of sympathy or the whole character of their civilisation being so different from ours, very few Europeans can spend more than a year amongst*

Chinese without suffering from it.[xlviii] Depression was particularly a problem amongst foreign women stationed there.

Towards the end of the 19th century and early 20th century, the number of foreign residents slowly began to increase, and foreigners were later permitted to reside on the central peninsula of Chongqing. Those that chose to do so, generally did so to be in proximity to their place of work, primarily missionaries and some diplomats and businessmen. But they were often confronted with poor quality living quarters.

In summer, most foreign residents would move across to the hills to the south of the Yangtze, some 700m above the main city, to escape slightly the searing heat of the Chongqing summers. Other foreign residents chose to live up on the hills all year round to hide themselves away from the "appalling filth and dirt" of the Chinese city around,

These hills remain dotted with fine European residences to this day but the impression of this European world apart has largely been lost due to the encroachment of the rapidly expanding city. Records of the time describe the two parallel ranges of the Nanshan (southern) hills here in a rather idyllic fashion.

Grace Service, wife of an American missionary, describes in the 1920s *"little valleys between the two ranges of hills [where] we saw the lovely blossoms of opium poppies which filled the small fields with their fragile grace. They gave the landscape beauty, but with a sinister threat to the public good"*[xlix]

This foreign world on the top of the mountain was a world apart from the city below. It was a community of missionaries, churches and Bible societies, Quaker schools and spacious bungalows with neat gardens, tennis courts and even a swimming pool – a rarity indeed in early 20th century inland China. For the foreign women residents, life was a series of visitors dropping in for afternoon tea, tiffin lunches at one of the few foreign clubs such as the American Oriental Bank's tiffin club, and the occasional school or church fete. The men often had to travel down to the south bank or across the Yangtze to the city centre for business, a journey of several hours by foot, sampan and sedan chair.

Such luxury provided a sharp contrast to the Chinese world around them. In the evenings there might be a concert where someone would sing, illuminated by Chinese lanterns hung in the trees around. The children flew kites, or explored the grave mounds that scattered the hills, daring each other to go and see where the earth had been washed away and left the bare coffin showing.

Occasionally residents went for a picnic on the river: Quaker family the Davidsons describe a day when they went to the hot springs on the gunboat HMS Widgeon where the sailors, whose lives had even less variety, made a great fuss of them.[1] There were also occasional Polo matches on a small sandbar in the middle of the Yangtze river near Longmenhao.

Community events were the highlight of an otherwise monotonous existence. The American community would organise a sports event and picnic to celebrate the 4th of July, to which the whole foreign community was invited. The American gunboat crew provided baked beans and ice cream. After supper there would be a programme in the school auditorium. A British businessman loaned a generator so there could be movies; an American businessman did some magic tricks. One hundred and thirty-five people were thought to have attended: quite a record for a foreign community event in Chungking. On another occasion missionary Grace Service commented:

"The sports program pleased both adults and children. But the movies scheduled for the evening had to be abandoned. The coolie bringing the portable generator apparently got lost. There were fireworks, however, that partially filled the gap in the program…. The sailors seemed to have a good time, and it was fine to have so many people of different nationalities picknicking and competing in sports together. No Germans came and no French. But we had Swedes, Russians, Hungarians, Letts, and plenty of British, with fine feeling throughout the gathering. We rented dishes and I personally had seen them washed and scalded, so I knew there was no danger of illness from that source."[li]

Elsewhere, there were Thanksgiving dinners at the American Oriental Bank's tiffin Club. The ladies furnished the dessert—mince and pumpkin pies with cheese—with candy, nuts, and coffee.

There was no cinema in Chungking in the 1920s so films were a great novelty. One of the British businessmen on the South Bank had a large house and a small electric generator. The YMCA had a portable projector and received films selected and circulated by the National Committee of the YMCA. The businessman would supply the electricity and the veranda; the YMCA would supply the projector and film; and the foreigners on the South Bank were invited to a free weekly movie.

Accommodation

Moving into a new house in the city in 1922, Grace Service describes the renovations needed to her kitchen to make it fit for purpose, including rat-proofing and screening involving massive sand filters arranged in tiers. Yangtze water was then strained through gravel, sand and finally charcoal.

Those travelling around China, for business or missionary work, were even less fortunate.

"The best conditions of Chinese inns", writes Edwin Dingle, *"are far and away worse than anything the traveller would be called upon to encounter anywhere in the British Isles, even in the most isolated places in rural Ireland. There can be no comparison. And my reader will understand that there is much which the European misses in the way of general physical comfort and cleanliness. Sanitation is absent in toto. Ordinary decency forbids one putting into print what the uninitiated traveller most desires to know--if he would be saved a severe shock at the outset; but everyone has to go through it, because one cannot write what one sees.*

All travellers who have had to put up at the caravanseries in Central and Western China will bear me out in my assertion that all of them reek with filth and are overrun by vermin of every description. The traveller whom misfortune has led to travel off the main roads of Russia may probably hesitate in expressing an opinion as to which country carries off the palm for unmitigated filth; but, with this exception, travellers in the Eastern Archipelago, in Central Asia, in Africa among the wildest tribes, are pretty well unanimous that compared with all these for dirt, disease, discomfort, an utter lack of decency and annoyance, the Chinese inn holds its own. And in no part of China more than in Szech'wan and Yün-nan is greater discomfort experienced". He goes on to describe a particularly memorable Yunnan establishment:

"It was truly a fearful den, where man and beast lived in promiscuous and insupportable filth. The dung-heap charms the sight of this agricultural people, without in the slightest wounding their olfactory nerves, and these utilitarians think there is no use seeking privacy to do what they regard as beneficial and productive work. The bed here was the worst I had had offered me. The mattress, upon which every previous traveller for many years had left his tribute of vermin, was not fit for use, there were myriads of filthy insects, and I found myself obliged to stop and have some clothes boiled, and for comfort's sake rubbed my body with Chinese wine."[lii]

Food

Getting supplies which foreigners considered necessities was difficult. At that time, as in many other parts of the world, many western travellers preferred to eat poor quality, but familiar food from tins rather than partake in any of the local cuisine. In the 1890s newcomers would typically bring six months of supplies with them packed in tin-lined cases, which often spoiled along the way. These would include items such as jam, marmalade, coffee beans, butter, baking and curry powder, Appollonaris water and large stores of wine and spirits.

When confronted with Chinese food, Europeans were generally unimpressed. Archibald Little described Chinese dinner parties as intolerably tedious affairs, combined with the absence of all real comfort.[liii] At that time, locals generally ate only two meals a day: breakfast at 10am and dinner around 5pm. Those that worked late, such as businessmen, who often spent their evenings smoking opium, sometimes fitted in an extra supper at 9pm to tidy them over until morning. Little described supper or "xiao ye" (small night) as *"another most unsatisfactory meal."[liv]*:

"By the light of an oil lamp we peck with our chopsticks at a few miniature dishes of cold onions, minced leeks, cold peas and beans, flavoured with vinegar and soy, apricot and melon seeds; all of which serve as a zest to numerous sups of mild hot rice wine (in reality a kind of beer; fermented not distilled)"

But Chinese food also had its fans amongst the more adventurous foreign travellers. Isabella Bird praised the enormous variety of Chinese food and its culinary art. She described the food as wholesome and well-cooked. But she said cleanly cooked and wholesome and excellent meals were often produced in dark and unsavoury surroundings and those foreigners who travel much in the interior *"learn to find Chinese food palatable."[lv]* Her chief objection to local food was the amount of vegetable oil used, and the prevalence of garlic and the strong flavour to the European palate of some of the vegetable oils much used, including castor oil, sesame and ground nut.

As today, the Chinese demonstrated little understanding of western tastes, despite often being keen to produce "European style" food to please foreign guests. Archibald Little describes meeting a Cantonese merchant called Chen who invites him to dine with him in a garden in the lower city. Chen promised a dinner cooked in the European style: having lived in the cosmopolitan cities of Shanghai and Canton he claimed to comprehend the wants of the barbarian appetite.

The dinner was "a decided failure", said Little: *"the strange meats were unacceptable to the other guests (all Chinese), and in order to show due appreciation of my host's hospitality, I had to make up for my fellow-guests' indifference by setting to as best I could.....Certainly if anything were needed to convince the company of their superior native refinement, as compared with our barbaric methods of eating, this feast was enough. In lieu of the chicken being neatly cut up, and stewed in a delicate sauce, all ready for serving to the mouth with the elegant chopsticks, a rough, plain boiled fowl was set on the table, with no carving knife to dissect it with.*

Each guest was provided with a miniature ivory-handled knife, and a two-pronged fork, and after much effort we succeeded in gnawing at fragments of the carcass, unaccompanied with bread or vegetables. Then came a leg of mutton roasted "rare", not bad in itself, but without potatoes and bread somewhat unpalatable. Little concluded: "After experience of this meal I began to think myself less a victim, than I did before, in being generally restricted in my travels to a Chinese cuisine pure and simple."[lvi]

The Chongqing of today abounds with similarly weird takes on western food. There are "western –style bakeries" filled with all manner of strange-looking oily cakes and buns with mixtures of sweet toppings, pork floss, ketchup and fake whipped cream (often combined). The city's newest Italian restaurant is proud to offer an interesting – to say the least - pear pizza.

Whether these bear any passing resemblance to western food seems unimportant. Locals knowing no better are happy with what they are served up, believing it to be an authentic western experience. They may leave comforted in the knowledge that Chinese food is indeed much better than those strange western concoctions... Today's western travellers in inland China also tend to conclude, as Archibald Little did, that it is far better to stick to local cuisine pure and simple than tolerate poor Chinese imitations of anything else.

Contact with locals

Early contact between English settlers and local residents in Chungking resulted in some extreme and wild rumours. Locals commented that they couldn't stand being in the proximity of foreigners because they smelt of "boiled meat" in the summer. Others reported they could smell the approach of a foreigner due to the quantity of dairy products foreigners were thought to consume. Writing from a small town in Yunnan province in 1910 Edwin Dingle says: *"a rumour is current in the town in which I am resting to the effect that foreigners are buying children and using their heads to oil the wheels of the new Yunnan railway"*

"Slay the foreigner!", was a common greeting to foreign residents on the rare occasions they dared to set foot in the streets. As a rule, foreigners learnt to be discreet, usually travelling everywhere in a closed sedan chair away from prying eyes. Those that were more adventurous often encountered trouble. As Edwin Dingle reports:

"a quiet jaunt through China on foot was, I was told, quite out of the question: the uneclipsed audacity of a man mentioning it was marvelled at. Did I not know that the foreigner must have a chair? Did I not know that no traveller in Western China, who at any rate had any sense of self-respect, would travel without a chair, not necessarily as a conveyance, but for the honour and glory of the thing? And did I not know

that, unfurnished with this undeniable token of respect, I should be liable to be thrust aside on the highway, to be kept waiting at ferries, to be relegated to the worst inn's worst room, and to be generally treated with indignity? The idea of mine of crossing China on foot was preposterous!"[lvii]

In spite of warnings that it was impossible for an English lady to walk in the streets of Chongqing, Alicia Little felt it impossible to live there unless she did. So after first trying several outings in sedan chair with the curtains up, unlike the other ladies who all kept theirs down, she decided to take a walk, with her sedan chair a short distance behind, to show she had at least some claim to respectability. She describes the event as follows:

"In a few minutes two or three hundred men and boys were following me. As long as they kept behind and did not press upon me, it did not so much matter; but the boys have a knack of clattering past, and then turning round to stare into one's face in the most insulting and annoying manner. And I felt I could not go back home with all this rabble following, as of course they would all try to press into our house after me, and there would probably be a row"[lviii]

When some local guards failed to help her, the only choice she could think of was to take out her camera and photograph the crowd and the guards not doing their duty. Then she got back in her chair and the crowd seemed satisfied that that was what she must have come for and soon dispersed.

Isabella Bird was an in fatigable Victorian traveller. Born the daughter of a Cheshire clergyman, she suffered from a spinal complaint in her early life and was sent to America and Canada in 1854 to improve her health. This is where her interest in travel was aroused.

In 1856 she published her first book, "An Englishwoman in America". She later went on to visit Australia, Hawaii, Japan, Malaya, Persia, Kurdistan, Korea and the wilds of inland China and Tibet, writing numerous further novels along the way, including "The Yangtze Valley and Beyond" in 1899.

She returned from the Far East in 1898 to make a final journey to Morocco at the age of seventy. She was extremely well-connected and well-respected for her travel writing, occasionally dining with Prime Minister Gladstone, meeting Queen Victoria, a well-known lecturer at the British Association and the Royal Geographical Society, and respected contributor to numerous learned journals. Her shrewd observations, perseverance and sheer courage made her an excellent travel writer, as entertaining and perceptive today as one hundred years ago.

China in particular fascinated her and given her Christian background, she claimed it was the country "in which her duty lay" and she spent considerable time visiting and reporting on the work of Christian missionaries there. Of all those who have travelled the Yangtze route over the ages, Isabella Bird's writings are considered to be amongst the classics.

Bird lists endless examples of mob attacks by locals on catching sight of a foreigner. There must have understandably been strong feelings towards foreigners for the way certain foreign countries took advantage of China's weak position in the late 19th and early 20th centuries to extract substantial commercial and territorial concessions from her. But these examples also highlight the gulf in understanding and experience between the Chinese and foreigners at that time and such attacks must have been a truly horrifying experience for early foreign settlers.

Indeed Bird herself never fully recovered from one particularly nasty attack where her sedan chair was forced open with a spade by an angry mob to chants of "foreign devil, "foreign dog" and "child eater", combined with kicks and spitting. She was struck on the head and *"suffered much for a long time from this blow and the brain disturbance that followed."[1]* When finally safely inside the inn in front of which this particular incident occurred, the wife of the innkeeper came to see Bird and spoke apologetically of the riot: *"if a foreign woman went to your country, you'd kill her, wouldn't you?"* [lix]

Sometimes the toughness of these situations became even too much for hardened travellers such as Bird. She writes in her diary one evening, after a particularly eventful arrival in a Sichuan trading town, complete with riots and being barred from several of the town's inns: *"Wretched evening; riotous crowd; everything anxious and odious; noises; too cold to sleep".* She continues: *"My lamp spluttered and went out, and my matches were too damp to strike. It is objectionable to be in the dark, you know not where, with walls absolutely precarious, and in the midst of the coarse shouts of rough men to hear feeble accompaniment of rats eating one's few things. I object strongly to a mixed crowd blocking up my doorway or breaking in my door, for every one of the crowd knows better; even the most ignorant coolie knows well that to intrude into a woman's room or in any way violate the privacy which is hers by immemorial usage and rigid etiquette is an outrage for which there is no forgiveness, judging from a Chinese standpoint."* [lx]

However extreme some of these tales seem, it is not hard to see some manifestations of this fear and wonder of foreigners even in today's China. In a modern metropolis such as Chongqing at the start of the 21st century, foreigners are still often greeted with a mixture of wonder and amusement. Locals often feel the need to broadcast the presence of a foreigner out loud for all to hear ("Laowai!") or one is pursued down the street with high pitched cries of "Helloooo!". It does not seem to matter if the utterer of the comment is seeing a foreigner for the first or the hundredth time: the reaction is the same.

The social scene

Those such as Isabella Bird and Alicia Little who sought out contact with the locals were confronted with the Chinese worldview, which proved, to say the least, surprising. Outside of China, it was believed there were five kingdoms united under one emperor, called Jesus Christ, who was of peasant origin. Of these five kingdoms, one was inhabited by dog-faced people (this was not intended as an insult, but the name used by the Chinese for a certain minority group); and in another each woman has two husbands and a hole in her chest and when the husbands travel, they put a pole through the hole and carry her!

On arrival in some towns, word would spread that a foreigner was in town and occasionally the local women submitted polite requests that the foreigner "show herself". The enormous size of Isabella Bird's feet was of great interest to one group, even though they were only size threes.

The shoe of even the poorest and most hard-worked Chinese peasant at that time never exceeded four inches in length. Big feet were considered vile and a Chinese girl with unbound feet would have no chance of marriage. They would ask questions such as *"what is your honourable age?"*, *"have you many sons?"*, *"why have you left your honourable country?"*. Then when tired of interrogating her, they would retreat into themselves, commenting on Bird's appearance: *"What ugly eyes she has, and straight eyebrows!"*, *"yes, but they see into the ground and where the gold is hid!", "has she come for the gold?", "what big feet she has!", "Why is her hair like wool?"*[lxi]

Edwin Dingle describes wandering into an inn in Yunnan: *"Everybody wondered, and softly asked his neighbour what in the sacred name of Confucius had come upon them, "See his boots! Look at his old hat! What a face! It is a monstrosity!"* [lxii]

Locals had never seen such things as lead pencils or fountain pens, foreign writing or indeed a woman writing so such things attracted great curiosity. A fork was regarded as a barbarism which would prick the mouth and make it bleed.[lxiii]

Alicia Little describes visits to the houses of rich local ladies and the niceties of Chinese visiting habits. *"One of the most fatiguing things about Chinese life is the presents.. whatever you do, you ought to take or send a present."* [lxiv]. The hostess would give presents for the guests' children; the hostess would pay for all her friends' chair coolies; and the guests would tip all of the hostess' servants, particularly the cook. The guests would also bring presents, usually sponge cakes or fruit, although on one occasion Alicia Little was offered a white cat. She describes the conversation at such gatherings as *"never very interesting"* but *"the chief fault in Chinese visits is that they are interminable."*[lxv]

Dress

European dress was a subject of great interest. Chinese ladies were greatly concerned about the decency of European women with their tight-laced bodices, petticoats and skirts. Chinese women always wore trousers and would often ask to examine under the petticoats of European women to check whether the rumour that they didn't wear trousers was really true. For the visit of a Viceroy to

Chongqing, all the city's foreigners were invited to attend, but were instructed to dress in Chinese clothes so as not to shock the populace by their queer foreign dress.

But some European women, such as Isabella Bird, saw Chinese dress as so comfortable and unrestrictive that she often preferred to adopt it over European dress. It also had the advantage of blunting the edge of curiosity of the locals and reduces the prodding and poking of local women touching and feeling foreign materials and styles. But she cleverly adapted her Chinese garb to the needs of a tireless traveller - attaching pockets in which she could conceal travel items, including a portable oil lamp, ready for use at a moment's notice; and a loaded revolver as a protection against robbers.

It was also difficult for westerners to keep up their standards of western attire in Szechwan's muggy, humid climate, with inadequate facilities. In the words of Grace Service: *"laundry work demanded much work and training of servants. It is quite a task to do up men's white summer suits, be they duck, silk, serge or flannel. I found the Szechwanese to be good washers, but poor rinsers. It was my rule to demand ample water for that use."[lxvi]*

Observations of the Chinese

These foreigners' close contact with the locals, enabled them to make some acute observations of the Chinese character and the monotonous rhythm of Chinese life at that time. The Chinese character is described as lazy, dull, disorganised, indifferent to suffering, and with little imagination. Isabella Bird said that the trivial questioning she was often subject to showed prodigious apathy on the part of local adults would *"spend hour after hour in focussing a stolid stare upon a person whose occupations offer no novelty or variety, being limited to eating or writing.*"[lxvii] Anyone who has lived for any length of time in China, can attest to similar sentiments today. A foreign walking down the street is a novelty, but a foreigner *cycling* down a street or *using chopsticks* attracts even greater attention and public comment!

Archibald Little said evenings in China were miserably dull: *"We sit about on hard square chairs, arranged in rows along the walls, and recreate ourselves by spitting the ash from the three-whiff hubble-bubble on the floor."*[lxviii]

A lacking of lighting in rural areas, and even in the city, prevented much other evening entertainment; a lack of newspapers or other reading material meant few but the literati found enjoyment in reading and literature; and there were few sporting or other fun activities to speak of. Many foreigners saw this as one of the principle reasons why opium had taken such a strong hold in China:

"What has he to gain by exerting himself? If he becomes rich, is not the life of a rich Chinaman so dull that only opium makes it possible to endure it? Once let Chinamen get a taste of the enjoyment of life, and they will be different people…; they get depressed, and hipped as we do; and they have no light literature, no sports, very little of a newspaper press, no picture galleries, no concerts, no bands, no intercourse with woman, except of the baser sort. No wonder they look dull. And how they love to be amused!"[lxix]

Alicia Little contrasted the leisure, fatigue and ennui of the women of the gentry and merchant classes with the incessant and hard demands on the lower classes. She was struck by the lack of learning and serious occupation of the women of the richer households of Chongqing in contrast to cities like Peking and Shanghai where daughters of rich families often shared their brothers' tutors and acquired literary skills.

Chongqing women of this class seemed to spend much of their leisure time looking after children, playing cards, gossiping, going to dinner parties or going on pilgrimages to distant shrines. They also regularly smoked opium. The women told Alicia that they usually took up the habit for reasons of poor health. Most sat up late into the night smoking and often did not get up until 5 or 6pm the next day.

At ladies' dinners, Little observed that the opium smokers tended to return from the opium couch with their eyes very bright, their cheeks very red and talking a great deal of nonsense very excitedly. Within a short space of time however, they looked yellow, sunken cheeked and most unhealthy. The women, she said, seemed no more ashamed of their habit than ladies were of drinking wine in Britain.

It was estimated that approximately 70% of all Chongqing men and 20% of women regularly smoked opium at that time. From being virtually unknown in western China in the 1850s, by the 1890s it was estimated there were more than 3000 opium dens in Chongqing alone. The opium pipe began to replace tea as the normal accompaniment of business discussions, and paper pipes were often placed on graves to enable the deceased to continue his or her dubious pleasures in the next world.

Footbinding

The Chinese practice of footbinding was considered one of

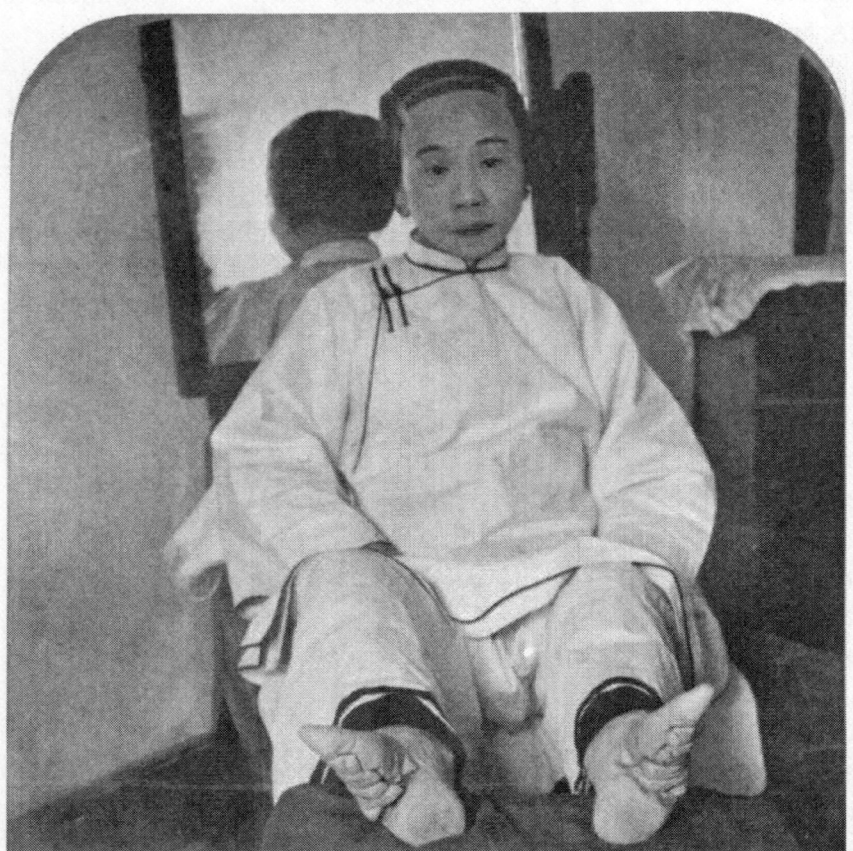

the few taboo subjects of conversation. The children of the rich usually had their feet bound between the ages of 4 and 5 years old, and the poor either at the time of marriage or between the ages of 7 and 9, depending on local custom. Usually, four of the toes were broken and doubled under the foot, then the big toe laid over the top. The deformity was then tightly bandaged and the bandaging repeated every day to ensure the "beauty" of the shape was not lost.

Bound feet were commonly referred to as "golden lilies" by the locals after a legend about Panfei, the favourite of

Emperor Hoti in the Qi Dynasty who was considered to be so beautiful that golden lilies sprang out of the ground wherever she stepped.

Directly after the binding, girls were made to walk on their aching feet to prevent mortification from immediately setting in. The following two years were the worst time for these girls as the foot is then no longer being narrowed but shortened by winding the bandages to draw the fleshy part of the foot and the heel closer together until it is possible to hide a coin between them. During this time, young girls presented a sorry picture, hobbling about with the help of a stick, being carried on a man's back or sitting sadly crying. Alicia Little described them as having great black lines under their eyes and a special curious paleness that she had never seen except in connection with footbinding.[lxx]

The only relief the girls had at their disposal was opium to forget the pain or from hanging their feet over the edge of the bedstead to stop the circulation. There was a Chinese saying that *"for each pair of bound feet there has been a whole kang, or big bath, of tears";* and one out of ten girls died from footbinding or its after-effects.

In one case treated by Dr McCartney of Chongqing, he removed a girl's binding to find both of her feet hanging by the tendons only with gangrene covering the whole of the feet above the ankles. Immediate amputation was necessary. He claimed the Chinese knew nothing of the physiology and anatomy of the human body and this ignorance causes untold suffering to the women and children of China.[lxxi]

Alicia Little felt strongly about this suffering and began to canvas support to bring a stop to the practice. This is considered by many commentators to be her greatest achievement: standing the women of China back on their feet.

In 1895 she founded the Natural Feet Society in Chongqing to raise awareness of the dangers of footbinding and campaign to bring a stop to the practice. To her surprise many foreign women in both Chongqing and Shanghai willingly volunteered to work on the Committee. They began by delivering tracts in Chinese featuring poems by Chinese women on the suffering they had experienced through footbinding. At first they doubted they would have any impact at all: *"to use the Chinese phrase, our hearts were very small indeed; for we knew the custom was so old, and the country so big. And what were we to fight against centuries and millions?"lxxii*

But a meeting in Chongqing brought them great hope. A number of local ladies and their children were invited to attend and arrived in their finest regalia. When told that in certain parts of China women didn't bind their feet, they became very animated and were keen to corroborate the facts. When told that on the road to Chengdu there was a town where a large proportion of the population inter-married and did not bind their feet because they were of Cantonese descent, the Cantonese ladies in the audience nodded and smiled knowingly. Then someone proffered that in parts of Hubei, neither rich nor poor bind, and two Hubei ladies in the audience spoke up and repeated the statement.

A foreign missionary explained the circulation of the blood with the aid of a length of rubber piping, showing the effects of binding. The ladies listened very tentatively followed by much questioning. The meeting resulted in all the women present agreeing that footbinding was of no use, but it could only be given up by degrees. The reaction of Chinese men was also interesting. Many of them admitted that none of their wives liked having their feet bound, and at another anti-footbinding meeting, all but six of the men present rose to their feet to express their opposition to footbinding.

Then Alicia Little's society had a stroke of luck. An examiner in the national civil service exam in Peking had to return to his home in Sichuan on the death of his father. On returning home, he witnessed the suffering of his seven-year-old daughter from her recently bound feet. During his trip from Peking to Chongqing, he had come across one of the Anti-footbinding society's tracts and he was compelled to act against his daughter's suffering. He ordered her feet be unbound; and furthermore, he set about writing an appeal to the nation on the subject of footbinding, which became known as the "Suifu (now Suining) Appeal".

He got five leading men of the neighbourhood to add their testimonies and names, then displayed it on the walls of the city of Suifu. Alicia's Natural Feet Society got hold of a copy thanks to foreign missionaries in Suifu and decided to use it to support their own campaigning efforts. They reprinted it and distributed the appeal to ten thousand students coming to Chongqing to sit the civil service exams. Then a letter arrived from the Shanghai manager of the China Merchants' Company, one of the great trading companies of China. He said he had heard of a wonderful tract against footbinding in the west and hoped to get hold of a copy to reprint at his own expense and distribute throughout his native province of Guangdong.

Slowly more and more important figures began to support the anti-footbinding movement. Kang, the Modern Sage and advisor to the Emperor, formed a No Bind Feet Society and attracted the support of Viceroys and high-ranking officials to pledge not to bind their daughters' feet and not to marry their sons to bound-feet girls.

Alicia Little's Natural Feet Society themselves wrote to the Empress Dowager on the subject to seek her support, writing in gold characters on white satin, enclosed in a silver casket. Finally, Duke Kang Hui-Chang, one of the lineal descendants of Confucius wrote to the Society:

"I have always had my unquiet thoughts about footbinding, and felt pity for the many sufferers. Yet I could not venture to say so publicly. Now there are happily certain benevolent gentlemen and virtuous daughters of ability, wise daughters from foreign lands, who have initiated a truly noble enterprise. They have addressed our women in animated exhortations, and founded a society for the prohibition of footbinding. They aim at extinguishing a pernicious custom."[lxxiii]

He then went on to apply for copies of their tracts so that he could compile a book of the best ones and circulate them further. Alicia Little and the Society were immensely proud of the phrase "wise daughters from foreign lands" and the fact that they achieved such a level of impact. In the space of two years, over 8000 poems, booklets and articles were written into support of natural feet and against footbinding, as a result of the work of the Natural Feet Society.

When Alicia visited England in 1898 and 1899, she was interviewed by a number of British newspapers and periodicals and gave speeches about her work on behalf of the Natural Feet Society. She also collected funds to further its work, including a fund-raising concert in Manchester. Little was considered a good organiser and speaker in support of the cause, often using humour to put across her most serious points.

Her efforts to help raise the profile of the anti footbinding movement in China had an impact on the attitude of Chinese communities outside China towards footbinding. The practice increasingly became viewed by Chinese officials, students and diplomats as an outmoded vestige of the past which made China appear "barbaric" or "half-civilised", thus causing some loss of international face. Many prominent Chinese reformers took up the issue of footbinding as part of their bid to strengthen and modernise China. In the last decade of the nineteenth century the leader of the reform movement, Kang Yu-Wei noted that in the eyes of foreigners nothing so much as footbinding made China appear so currently backward:

"There is nothing which makes us objects of ridicule so much as footbinding.. With prosperity so weakened, how can we engage in battle? I look at the Europeans and Americans, so strong and vigorous because their mothers do not bind their feet and therefore have strong offspring. Now that we must compete with other nations, to transmit weak offspring is perilous."[lxxiv]

Footbinding was finally outlawed in China in 1912, on the arrival to power of the Nationalists. In 1907 Alicia and Archibald Little returned to England and Alicia continued to write and speak on China to British audiences and campaign for women's rights.

She protested alongside Emily Pankhurst in favour of votes for women, and for women to retain their rights to their own wealth and property after marriage – both causes she felt particularly strongly about.

At the turn of the century no other European woman or organisation had played such a public role in Chinese affairs or was to intervene so fundamentally in the domestic and social lives of Chinese women. She is also equally well-known today by European students of China for her written records of the domestic and social lives of the Chinese with whom *"I have lived on somewhat intimate terms for eleven years."*

Modernisation

The late 1920s brought significant change to Chungking. The country was modernising and signs of this finally arrived in western China, fuelled by the return of students from other parts of China. Streets were widened, new and better buildings went up, an electric-light plant capable of twenty-four-hour industrial service was built, as was a piped water system, and adequate telephone exchange.

In a city where no wheeled transport was in regular use inside the city walls until 1927, the widening of the streets brought big changes. Pavements were constructed exclusively for pedestrian use, with the aim of leaving the roads clear for the new wheeled traffic. Tuk-tuks, carts, automobiles, and bicycles shared the streets with coolies and sedan chairs.

Shop fronts were modernised and sometimes westernised: a glazed-brick-veneer front in "modern" design could conceal a centuries-old interior with beautifully carved wooden panelling and bare, carved supporting timbers. Buildings began to get taller: new building materials meant that buildings were reaching seven storeys in the late 1920s and neon-light advertising began to be seen illuminating larger shops, offices, and buildings.

Electric-light and telephone poles cluttered the streets, and military telephone lines, insecurely strung, added greatly to the visual confusion. Several art-deco style buildings from this period remain in the city today, although in an advanced state of decay.

There was to be another influx of foreigners to Chongqing during the Second World War when Chongqing briefly became the capital of China and the city suffered the dubious award of becoming the most heavily bombed city in the history of the world.

The bombing led many local wealthier families to vacate the city centre for villages on the city's edge, prompting the beginning of the urban expansion of the city towards the megapolis it has become today. Their places were soon taken in the city centre by newly arrived evacuees from other parts of China as the Nationalist government moved its universities, factories and government functions westward, out of reach of the Japanese. New foreign residents included journalists reporting from the wartime capital, foreign soldiers, and diplomats.

This influx of foreigners created what seems to have been an altogether more international city than Chongqing even today. Robert Payne describes Chungking as having all the modern conveniences. There were skyscrapers, some even with lifts, black shining limousines, flower vendors and steam ships. A modern press building in Lianglukou housed foreign journalists who had come to report on the war and Chinese resistance to it. There was even a dairy, which sold excellent milk at exorbitant prices.[lxxv] And a trend for ice cream parlours - every street corner had one: *"in small rooms, painted blue, with electric fans whirring pleasantly, in a temperature of 80 degrees, we drink iced lemonade."*[lxxvi]

There was an active cultural scene, although this was being severely limited by the war. The cinemas that there were had received no new films since the loss of access through the Burma Road. So entertainment consisted mainly of damaged pre-vintage American films played in dark theatres. There were also plays, for example about the life of Mozart, or the work of the Chinese Red Cross.

The city had four or five good western restaurants, including the "Daisy" and "Moscow", both owned by Russian émigrés. An American naval officer based in the city recalls the American naval boat USS Tutuila where he used to go for "a good curry". It had been more or less a permanent fixture at the quayside in Chungking, marooned there by the Japanese occupation further downstream[lxxvii].

Robert Payne describes the atmosphere of the Chungking Club in wartime Chungking:

"Sitting among the black leather armchairs, uncomfortably manoeuvring against the broken springs, you can watch the foreign population off their guard. There are the fanatical bridge players, two young Jews whispering in a corner, the wife of an insurance agent, three or four Customs officials, the soldiers and the sailors.. Missionaries who have taken to business, armament vendors, dope smugglers… You come upon a man who is white-haired and holds himself stiffly as he drinks his last glass of the extremely potent drink which is known as "Chungking gin".

He describes a world in which the values of Shanghai had suddenly been transplanted to Chungking, given the huge numbers of refugees from eastern China who flooded to the city during the war years:

"It is curious to notice how many of the shops describe themselves as coming from Shanghai… To get rich quickly, to have a mistress.. to be able to give dinners in which shark's fin, already almost unobtainable, will be served as a delicacy; to ride in motor cars and be able to say your income can be measured in millions are the hallmarks of the most exquisite taste. The old Chinese scholars have temporarily vanished, or they are hiding in small hotel bedrooms on larger than a cupboard." These values are now commonplace in modern China: the values of once decadent Shanghai have become the norm".

With the blockade of the city, inflation was a growing problem. On Monday an orangeade might cost fifteen dollars; on Tuesday it was twenty; on Thursday it was thirty. *"So does everything rise, and we sit in corners discussing the inflation."[lxxviii]* Later he says: *"I have been making a comparative list of prices. Two years ago in Chungking I could eat reasonably well for USD 300 a month. Today I eat less and it costs USD 3000 a month. Two years ago one could buy a fountain pen for thirty dollars. Today it costs USD 700. And so with everything else – a pencil costs USD 80, which is equivalent to a pound sterling or four or five dollars gold. A typewriter costs USD 150,000, which is equivalent to 2000 pounds. A small house will costs USD 3 million, which is equivalent, at the official exchange rate, to over 30,000 pounds. No one can foretell what the next month will bring in a sudden leap of prices. The spiral goes higher. What happens when it reaches the sun?"[lxxix]*

Aside from the above influences of modernity, the old Chungking lived on in parallel, and evidence of the damage of war was everywhere. Rubble was strewn about the streets. Side streets off main thoroughfares led to nowhere.

Many shop fronts were not much more than facades, and as you walked through them, out into the courtyard on the other side, rubble faced you again. The solidity of ancient China was absent here: everything was flimsy and temporary. Shopkeepers often scribbled on the thin plaster walls in clumsy Chinese characters, almost illegible, the names of the proprietors and the wares they were selling.

As seen in Chapter 3, shortly after the end of the Second World War the majority of British and western residents in western China fled the country and China's more or less closed its doors to western influence. Nevertheless, it was perhaps in the field of lifestyle and culture that early British settlers and travellers had the greatest lasting influence in western China.

Many of the people cited in this chapter were the first to record in the English language testimonials of everyday life in 19th and early 20th century China. Some of these have proved of lasting literary value, including the accounts of Somerset Maugham and Isabella Bird. They paint a vivid picture of a society on the brink of change as it came into contact with western civilisation for the first time, including the hostilities, bewilderment and unwanted interest they had to deal with from locals.

These early British residents and travellers planted the seeds of lasting western influence on Chinese tastes, fashions and architecture. This started with small things such as Lancashire woollen yarn used to tie ladies' hair, and the popularity of British cigarettes and umbrellas, but has now grown to such a degree that nowadays most young Chinese would consider most fashions, gadgets and design of western origin as preferable to their Chinese counterparts.

Chapter 5:

<u>Religion and Education</u>

"The pioneers do not always go .. in lust of land; sometimes they go to satisfy their souls"

William Allen White

No foreigners experienced the full brunt of life in 19th and early 20th century China more than missionaries.

Due to the nature of their work, missionaries usually chose to live and dress like locals. They settled in the remotest of places with no western comforts, unfamiliar food and no friendly faces around. When they travelled, they did so in the most primitive conditions, and faced daily hostilities and curiosity wherever they went.

Many missionaries were fresh-faced young people with little or no previous experience of overseas travel, and little idea of the type of conditions they would be expected to endure in remote corners of China. For these reasons, their memoirs and writings give a heightened impression of the gap in civilisations between east and west at that time.

Christian missionaries were by far the most numerous foreigners in China during the nineteenth and early twentieth centuries, profiting the most from the opening up of inland areas and right to travel provided by the treaties. Missionaries were fired by an enthusiastic fundamentalist belief and concern for the conversion of pagan souls, where China presented enormous possibilities.

Most Christian denominations were represented, including Anglicans, Methodists, Quakers, Baptists and Seventh Day Adventists. As Robert Davidson, a Quaker missionary who spent much of his life in Chungking put it: *"What can we do amongst so many? One fifth of the population of London [in one small town in Sichuan] and not a witness for the Lord Jesus? When I think of it I am simply overpowered... If a man were drowning and called for help it would be a sin if nothing were done to save. Yet here men are as it were drowned by idolatry, superstition and sin".*[lxxx]

For many Chinese, their first contact with a foreigner was with a missionary, and as such, missionaries came to be the most despised by locals. *"Take away your opium and your missionaries and you will be welcome,"* said Prince Kung to the British Ambassador in 1869.

The Chinese saw themselves less as a nation-state than a civilisation, based on the teachings of Confucius and the Sages. The guardians and propagators of these teachings were the scholar-gentry, the dominant social class, whose status, in theory at least, was dependent on learning rather than wealth. All officials came from this class, and entry into it was achieved by success in the civil service examinations in classical literature, a system which had existed in some form for over a thousand years.

But by the nineteenth century the system provided a barrier to changes which contact with the West necessitated. The missionary, with his teachings, challenged the cultural dominance of the scholar-gentry; and he challenged their social power. With his rights of direct access to officials, and power to appeal over their heads to his ambassador in Peking, he seemed to undermine the whole structure of Chinese civilisation[lxxxi].

The French were the early pioneers of missionary work in China. Catholic mission work had begun as early as the late 16th century; in the 18th century it had been forbidden, but the French had continued clandestinely. Sichuan was the province where Catholic mission work had been the most successful, and by 1870 there were an estimated 80,000 Catholic converts there, out of 400,000 in the whole of China.

In contrast, there were fewer than 6000 Chinese Protestants, though the first Protestant missionary, Robert Morrison had begun work in 1809. Although the two branches of Christianity went under different names, to the average Chinese the distinction was unimportant; and the numerical predominance of Catholics in the 19th century meant that the behaviour of Catholic missionaries determined Chinese attitudes towards the foreign religion.

The Chinese in general had a laissez faire attitude to the main religions of China: Confucianism, Buddhism and Taoism. By the 19th century, most Chinese would say that they followed the "three doctrines", and worshipped indiscriminately in temples of each cult. Even Chinese Muslims seemed to have accommodated themselves into this laissez-faire attitude to some extent. But Christianity entailed not only preaching one's own doctrine, but opposing all others. It is not hard to sympathise with the Confucians when one reads the glee with which missionaries report the burning of idols or ancestral tablets by their converts, or how they have persuaded vegetarian Buddhists to eat meat.

When Christians preached morality, this was well accepted and well understood by the Chinese; but the heart of their creed, concepts such as sin, salvation, conversion, atonement and above all the exclusiveness of Christianity, were utterly alien to their audience. In the worlds of one local: *we like your Jesus, he is a good man, just like Confucius, both good men. We don't mind you telling us about Jesus, but why do you stop us worshipping our ancestors?"*

A Chinese who destroyed his ancestral tablets was cutting himself off from all decent society; conversion entailed refusing other basic social duties such as the upkeep of local temples. As a result, true converts to Christianity were few, and those that existed were usually amongst the poor and uneducated. The educated were almost without exception hostile, and those who knew the history of the opium wars felt that the British and other foreigners had little right to preach morality to the Chinese.[lxxxii]

One problem missionaries encountered in getting their message through to the locals was vocabulary. The only term that evoked any response was "good deeds". There seemed no distinction between "heaven and earth" and "maker of heaven and earth" in Chinese, and no real equivalent for "God", "soul" or "creator". "Sin" was often understood as "debt". The promise of release from that too-common burden certainly aroused interest and hope – and swift disillusionment. Another barrier was Chinese courtesy; *"the Chinese man or woman will generally agree with all one says while not really believing a word."*[lxxxiii]

Anti-Christian riots were common across China, but particularly in Sichuan with its high concentration of missionaries. These riots were often fomented by the scholar-gentry, and helped to spread anti-Christian literature of scurrilous and bizarre rumours about missionaries and their converts.

These rumours included the rampant sexual behaviour of missionaries and their converts; that missionaries were all spies for western governments; and that the western medicine which they practiced had as its goal to gorge out the eyes of Chinese children and mix them with lead to convert it to silver.

Isabella Bird describes an incident involving missionaries in the town of Wanzhou, typical of the incomprehension that existed at the time:

"On another occasion, a well ran dry in the town of Wanzhou and locals immediately blamed a couple of missionaries stationed in the town for tapping the well in order to steal the golden crab which was the "luck" of the city. Then a mandarin was brought to the house with a serious charge that the missionaries had killed children in order to get their eyes – commonly believed to be used by foreigners in medicine - , and that their bodies were in the water tanks at the back of the house. The tanks were probed with a long pole with no result, but the angry locals were still unsatisfied, "for the foreign magic is believed to be equal to anything." [lxxxiv] *Missionaries were accused of occupying houses for hellish purposes, digging under them to make a way to England so that foreign soldiers could then come to China through the tunnel to take Chinese land. It was also said they wanted lock-up rooms in which to hide the golden cocks which they dug out of the mountains by night!"* [lxxxv]

Christians lived in a state of constant fear of attack and abuse. In light of this, it is surprising how peaceful and unmolested the lives of most missionaries' were, in their tiny communities scattered throughout the Empire, miles from any compatriots and the protective presence of foreign gunboats; and the dedication they showed to their task. The locals might be hostile, but they could also be friendly and hospitable, and anyone who knows the Chinese knows they have an inexhaustible curiosity, particularly when it comes to foreigners. What perhaps saved the missionary most was the Chinese sense of humour, and the food for it provided by these foreigners with their ludicrous appearance, customs and beliefs.

Other members of foreign communities also largely saw missionaries as a nuisance. The British authorities often saw the missionaries as stirring up trouble and thus damaging trade, but they were obliged to protect their own citizens in case of danger.

An attack against a group of Chungking-based Quakers in the late 1890s illustrates the dichotomy of viewpoint between missionaries and British consular staff. Quaker Robert Warburton was attacked by an angry mob visiting a small market town outside Chungking – the first foreigner ever to set foot there.

Robert survived intact, but the British Consul insisted in using the incident as an example of the growing violence against Europeans in western China, and insisted on punishing the local officials for not carrying out their duty under the Treaties to protect foreign nationals within China. The pacifist Quakers argued that they were not looking for vengeance and simply wanted friendly relations with the local community. But the Consul won and those involved in the assault were punished, the Quakers were compensated, and the Prefect ordered to donate money towards the building of a mission hospital in Tungchwan and a house for a street chapel in Yulungchen.

Alicia Little, in her book, "intimate China", describes a typical conversation within the foreign community about missionaries, oscillating between ridicule and admiration for the hardships they endured:

"The prejudice against missionaries is really one of the most amusing things in China. They all hang about Chefoo. That

is the sort of place that suits them. A nice comfortable house, and nothing to do! Just about suit me too! I'd like to find a merchant's clerk who did as little as one of these self-devoted men, who have given up everything" is a little speech I heard one man make to three others one day, *apparently expressing the sentiments and experience of all"*

Then the conversation moves on to individuals who stand out from the rest: *"Oh, Dr Nevius! Oh! But he's quite an exceptional man. He does more good than all the others put together, I believe......Mr. Barber!..A University man! Seventeenth Wrangler you know, and a splendid all round man – good at cricket, and football, and everything..... Mr Hill! You won't meet another man like him in a hurry!"*

Alicia Little goes on to say:

"Thus the conversation goes on about pretty well every missionary any one knows anything about; and yet winds up as it began: "But the missionaries generally are quite different, - and hang about and make believe – and save money – and go home!" These typical missionaries no one seems ever to have met; yet everyone who has been to China must agree one hears plenty about them. It begins on the voyage out, when you are told about the poor girls – the enthusiastic, misguided young girls they lure out to wretchedness, nobody knows where. "Clap them into Chinese dress the moment they arrive, and send them off up-country, where there is not a single European, in carts and all sorts of miserable conveyances. That's what they do. Why the poor girls don't know themselves where they are going to."lxxxvi

In Alicia's case, one small incident had convinced her of one of the benefits the missionaries were bringing to Chungking.

Visiting a Christian school in the city one day she concluded that the western teaching methods the missionaries brought with them were of real benefit to locals:

"I was surprised when the first class, being led up to an outline map of Africa without names, called out Congoland, Madagascar, Natal and the like as the examiner pointed. They did the same by Asia….If into these little girls' heads it really had penetrated that there were other kingdoms in the world besides their own, they were in so far better taught than most of the literati of the land, and no knowledge would seem more to be desired for a Chinaman just now…..But what struck me most was the expressions of the children. They were interesting, they were attractive, simply because the mind in them evidently had been aroused, and was working. The blank, dead-wall Chinese stolidity was gone."

For their part, the missionaries also held their opinions of the remainder of the expat population of businessmen, officials and their families. European businessmen were criticised for leading *"a rollicking life of drink, gambling and lust"*. The growth of the foreign business community after 1900 was a source of great embarrassment to missionaries who found it harder to pretend, even to themselves, that they came from a morally superior, because Christian, civilisation. Everything a foreigner did was known to the Chinese, and a man "of immoral life" could not pass undetected; but if missionaries tried to keep their distance from such a man and were unwise enough to say why, they were threatened with acts of slander."

The realities of missionary work in Western China

Day-to-day missionary work consisted of a number of activities: opportunistic preaching or "itinerating" where missionaries travelled from town to town selling tracts and preaching in market places or wherever they could find an audience; services; medical work; education; and later campaigning against certain causes, or other sidelines where they thought they could add value to the local community.

Quaker Robert Davidson describes his first experience of itinerating thus. He and colleagues stopped in a village and raised their ti-mu – a scroll of red calico with a text written in black characters – and began to speak to the crowd that would inevitably gather. The text would frequently be changed to maintain interest, and it was also needed to supplement the speaker's inadequate broken Chinese.

Robert could not yet speak in public, but one evening at the inn some men came in for medical treatment, and he decide to deliver his first sermon in basic Chinese:

"Many a time when at home I wished to know how people spoke to the heathen and I am not surprised to find the difficulty of reaching them.. The crowd is composed chiefly of men, scarcely a women to be seen.. Two lonely foreigners, standing in a crowd of Chinese, whose first and last thoughts are chiefly of their cash, do not find their position one of the easiest. After all one's efforts, how trying it is to get a sudden remark about the colour of one's eyes, or the socks one wears..."

And occasionally there was open hostility: *"one day a respectable looking man came up and said, "We hate you English. We hate your Jesus"* and stamping his feet added, *"We would do that with him", and ground his teeth."* This kind of incident gave a much truer picture of missionary life that the descriptions usually found in missionary magazines of the day.[lxxxvii]

As missionaries became more experienced in the ways of the Chinese, they often adopted their approach to itinerating in an attempt to get better results. On his first itinerating trip outside Chungking to the rural towns of Sichuan province, Robert Davidson's assistant, a Sichuanese called Hsieh, advised him:

"we must remember we come as strangers. If at the very first we declare to the people that they are all wrong, their gods false, the traditions of their fathers errors, the worship which they have had for centuries useless, we offend them, and in many cases it is like hitting a man a slap across the mouth, it raises their passion. Their ideas of "slowly, slowly" have in some measure to be complied with. Some missionaries go straight away and preach against idolatry in the streets. If we would win the people, we must respect their prejudices a little, and give way to their ideas in some things. The best way is individual personal contact".

The Sichuanese were very fond of "t'an hsien" in the evenings – a Chinese expression for gossip and conversation. Robert therefore left it to Hsieh to tell his fellow townsmen something of Robert's intentions, and of his medical skills, while Robert himself walked about the streets, sat in teahouses, and struck up conversations with people, making no effort to evangelise, but just trying to create a friendly atmosphere.[lxxxviii]

Female missionaries were never allowed to forget the inferior position of women in China, and had to be continually alert to the dangers of causing scandal. Walking through the streets of Chungking, Mary-Jane Davidson had to keep several paces behind her husband Robert, and no other male missionary would dare to be seen accompanying her. She never shook a male colleague by the hand, or sat on the same side of the table at mealtimes.

Medical work was by far the most successful area of work for most missionaries, giving them close contact with ordinary people. It was mainly the poorer classes who went to the missionaries for medical help, but as they got better known their help was occasionally sought even by the magistrate's "yamen" or official residence.

Although suspicion of western medicine was high, the missionaries' dispensary work had an obviously benevolent purpose that could be understood in Confucian terms, and gave them an excuse for their presence. The missionaries' real purpose was quite incomprehensible, and it was assumed that he must be an agent of a European power spying on the local area. More vicious rumours saw all foreigners as "child eaters" and children routinely had crosses sewn into their clothing to protect them from the dangerous foreigners.[lxxxix]

Missionaries did not charge for medical treatment, except for opium cures, but were often rewarded with gifts of money, clothing or food. So they got to know people better and won their good will; and at the same time had a captive audience in the waiting room, where the Chinese assistant used the time to talk about the Gospel.

At the Quaker Friends Mission in Chungking, over 2000 patients were seen at the dispensary in the first 3 months of operation, sometimes as many as 80 in a single morning. For example, a poor woman called Chen who came to the dispensary with a pain in her side, which was wonderfully eased, she said, by the medicine prescribed. Every day she returned for the medicine, and even when her pain was gone, she returned to hear the preaching: *"If the foreigners' medicine is good, their Tao-li (doctrine) may be good too"* she said.

Eventually she confessed her faith in Christ, and asked Mary-Jane to visit her home to witness the burning of her idols. Afterwards, Mary-Jane told Gospel stories and showed pictures to the neighbours who had gathered outside. Chen's faith seems to have endured, whatever it meant to her: she was still a member of the Church ten years later.

Many of the missionaries had only basic medical training – barefoot doctors before their time – and many patients came with incurable diseases they could do little for. But the majority could perform simple medical tasks such as setting broken limbs, prescribing quinine and other western medicines, treating eye infections and so on.

But there were psychological ailments too which missionaries were culturally hardly equipped to handle: the woman suffering from temporary insanity after her husband had cursed her for not performing the New Year ceremonies properly; and Mr. T'sao who had a breakdown after failing the Civil Service examinations and burst into tears at the sight of a book.

Then there was opium poisoning, for which every British missionary in China felt a peculiar responsibility. Forty years earlier opium had been virtually unknown in Sichuan, but by the 1890s there were more than 3000 dens in Chungking alone. Estimates of smokers varied from 50 – 80% of men in cities, and at least 20% of the women. In the countryside there were fewer, but even there, in this fertile landscape, could be seen the pale faces and emaciated bodies of addicts.

More and more of Sichuanese soil was being turned over to the cultivation of the poppy, and opium was now, after silk, the most valuable Sichuanese export. Universally, the Chinese recognised the evil of opium and wanted to renounce it, yet the capacity for resistance was lacking, and there were now powerful commercial interests in its favour. The opium pipe was coming to replace tea as the normal accompaniment of business discussions, and paper pipes could be seen on graves, to enable the deceased to continue his dubious pleasures in the next world. Missionaries did what they could to help those suffering from addiction or poisoning. Some were sent to opium refuges, such as that run by the Christian Inland Mission in Chungking. Others were treated with quinine and "a little oversight".

In 1890 the Quaker Friends Missions rented a spacious three-courtyard house on White Dragon Fountain Street in Chungking to open their first city mission. Over the main entrance was a lacquered black board with the gold characters Fu Yin Tang – Good News Hall. In the first courtyard was a dispensary, a schoolroom, and guestrooms for men and women. In the second courtyard was a preaching hall, decorated with scrolls giving the Ten Commandments, the Lord's Prayer and, interestingly, Confucius' Golden Rule. The living accommodation was in the third courtyard. The mission was run by Robert Davidson and his wife Mary-Jane, and Caroline Southall. All the neighbours, of course, would have assumed that Caroline was Robert's secondary wife, and have commented on the discrepancy between these foreigners' preaching and their practice.

A traditional feast marked the opening of the mission on 3 March 1890. The neighbours sent presents of oranges and sweetmeats and there were 120 guests in total, including the builders who had been working on the house, and according to custom, the chief robber and a couple of leading beggars, to ward off theft and unwanted visitors.

The guests sat at little square tables, starting with shrimps, dates, and melon seeds, and moving on to chicken, pork, duck, sweet rice balls, boiled seaweed and rice. Robert went from table to table bowing and making formal apologies for the poor and inadequate food. The Chinese love a social occasion and Robert revelled in the atmosphere.

The next day they held a service of dedication, attended by at least 300 people, many having to stand in the courtyard outside. As the days went on, crowds continued to gather in the street outside the mission out of curiosity rather than reverence. They pushed forward to catch a glimpse of Mary-Jane playing the harmonium, pulled at Caroline's clothes while she urged them to listen to Robert's preaching, and during prayers some bolder spirits amongst the men stood on chairs to peer over the partition into the women's section, filled with glee at what they saw. It was hard to get anyone to leave, and left the missionaries feeling overwhelmed. They considered telegraphing London for help, but decided that no one would understand the depiction of life in Chungking that they would paint.

Soon, however, they fell into the routine daily life of a city mission. There were 2 services every Sunday, a men's meeting on Wednesday evenings, women's Bible study on

Thursday mornings, preaching to passers-by on Tuesday and Thursday mornings, and dispensary work on Monday, Wednesday and Friday mornings. In addition to this the missionaries had to fit in Bible study, language study, and constant socialising with foreigners and local Chinese.

Services consisted of preaching, Bible readings, singing and prayers. Yet they bore little relation to church services at home. People bustled in and out, and chattered and commented throughout, in the manner of all Chinese audiences. Robert commented how:

"some dart in with a meaning smile as if they have at last struck something really funny and are determined to sit it out; collies lift heavy burdens from their tired shoulders and rest a while; others plump down baskets in the nearest corner and listen. Wretched looking beggars, almost nude and carrying a dirty rice bowl, creep in and perhaps sit beside some well-dressed fellow.

Now and then a Buddhist priest, with shaven head full of burnt scars, will come shuffling in...I noticed one admiring himself and arranging his toilet, using our polished door as a mirror. Another touches the wall with his fingers or tries to peer into the plaster as if everything connected with foreigners must be intrinsically wonderful."[xc]

Gradually though, the novelty wore off and a few could be recognised as repeating their visits and paying attention to what was said. All missionaries found though that true converts were hard to come by. The first to show interest in the Quakers were two of their own servants, but there was always a shadow over the sincerity of those whose livelihood depended on the mission, for whom it was an "iron rice bowl".

Yet as Robert Davidson reported defensively, if they couldn't even influence their own servants, what hope did they have with the others?". Li Ling-lin and Chang Yu-lin became the first Chinese Quakers in April 1891 and remained faithful. Chang's was the first Chinese Quaker wedding in 1894, and he was last heard of in 1911 still working as an evangelist in the Sichuan town of Tungliang.

On the whole though, it was frustrating work. The Chinese seemed frustratingly contented with their lives, conscious of no spiritual needs, and quite happy to exist on a wholly material level. Sometimes the frustration of it all would become too much for the missionaries. *"Sometimes it seems awfully hopeless work",* wrote Mary-Jane in her diary.

Following a bad experience with a hostile crowd, Warburton, another of the Quaker mission wrote: *"As I sat in the darkness listening to the hum of that crowd and the dismal wail of the singers, the terrible darkness of heathenism seemed to creep over me like a nightmare, and I could not restrain the tears from trickling down my face. When a man realises he is shut off from all his kind, amid scenes like these, when the last words he has heard from then man he wants to help and save are "beat him, kill him", he understands as never before Gethsemane and the drops of blood".* The next day Warburton felt too ill to continue, and returned to the nearest town and *"thanked God for the sight of an Englishman."*[xci]

Robert Davidson describes one trip to the Tungchwan area of Sichuan as a *"tragic-comedy of incomprehension".* Quaker missionaries had been working in the area for a while and there seemed to be much interest in Robert's arrival. In Yulungchen 48 enquirers gathered, varied in their intellectual level and social background. Robert examined them one by one and got some strange answers: *"Who is God? – "Jesus Lao Ren – Jesus Old Man"; "Why do you come to the church?" – "Because my name will be taken to England".*

Later Robert wrote: *"the way these people attach themselves to the Christians without the slightest knowledge of what they are doing, is almost incomprehensible to a foreigner. Some of them told me they believed the doctrine, but when asked what the doctrine was, they pleaded entire ignorance, some even not knowing the name of the God we worship, and yet they say they had been joined to the Christians and had attended meetings for a year."*[xcii]

It soon became clear that many answers lay in the political background to the time. Many Chinese believed that foreign governments might offer them protection if they signed up to the *"foreign religion"*. The French government offered the same protection to Catholic converts as it is did to French nationals in China. Some hoped the British government might do the same for Protestants.

There was common talk in China and abroad at that time that the imperial powers were planning to divide up China "like a melon" into different spheres of influence. It was said that the Catholics in Guizhou province had been openly telling people that they should join the Church at once, before the French arrived from Indo-China. And then there were those who looked on the Church as a kind of secret society – a potent source of protection – and the prayers and worship were merely the rituals which all such societies went in for. In the end, perhaps one in fifty of those who flocked into the Church in those years had any understanding of what it was really all about.[xciii]

There was also incomprehension of the conditions in which missionaries lived back in their funding institutions in Britain. There were constant questions from London about unnecessary expenses, lack of progress in recruiting new members and inflexible rules to deal with, such as missionaries not being able to marry while on a posting. This only added to the frustrations the missionaries had to face.

Family Life

The life of Protestant missionaries in China was of course very different to that of Catholics, given that Protestants were usually accompanied by their partner and children. Protestant missionaries might theoretically be prepared to endure all kinds of discomfort or danger, but felt they had no right to impose this on their children. So they often built themselves large, airy houses in the cities; they had bungalows on the hills for the summer time; and every few years went home on furlough, deserting their missionary work for a year or more. They employed servants, at very least a cook, houseboy, tableboy, chairman and one or two amahs – nannies - for the children. The belief died hard that Chinese food and western digestions were incompatible, so they lived off tinned food imported at great cost from Shanghai.

The Davidson family children were brought up with Chinese as their first language, although English was required at mealtimes. Their amahs told them Chinese legends, of dragons and snake spirits, and taught them children's songs. Occasionally they sneaked into the servants' quarters and were given a taste of their delicious but forbidden food, much nicer than the scrawny chicken and tinned beans they were used to. Speaking Chinese like natives, they could sometimes help their parents when there was a language problem.

Education

It was in the field of education that the missionaries probably had the longest lasting impact on life in western China. Indeed, some of their educational institutions, including the Friends High School in Chungking and the Western Union University in Chengdu continue to thrive to this day, well into their second century of existence.

Missionary schools offered basic education to poor Chinese, both boys and girls. At the time, such children would otherwise have received no formal schooling, therefore traditional Chinese teachers viewed the mission schools with considerable suspicion. The missionaries' main purpose was, of course, to inculcate Christian ideas, but Quakers were also committed to imparting "western learning" and new attitudes towards education.

The traditional Chinese school was based around learning by rote, the children shouting out the sounds of characters until they had been memorised, with little concern for their meaning. There was little discipline either: missionary literature was full of descriptions of the classroom as "bear gardens" and the children as "Babels".

The missionaries could do little to affect the teaching of Chinese, but they gradually introduced new subjects and attitudes. The children learnt that they need not bring incense sticks or paper money for the school God; and when they were introduced to Christian literature they were taught the meaning as well as the sound of the characters. At this point, some were removed from the school by their parents.

New subjects introduced included Geography, Bible history, arithmetic with Arabic numerals and singing. Prizes were also given for punctuality to encourage a disciplined approach to learning. Other European imports included slates and pencils, desks all facing one way to encourage discipline, and a harmonium and magic lantern – the latter often used in evangelistic work.[xciv]

The Quakers established their first school in Chungking in February 1891 – a girl's school. The very idea of educating girls at that time was revolutionary: *"Women don't count in China"* wrote Many-Jane Davidson, *"Boys count as children, girls are only girls"*. About 25 girls came initially but most didn't stay long, and at the age of thirteen they were all confined to their homes until their marriage.

Source:

A boys' school opened in Chungking a year later, and was to become one of the Quakers' most important enterprises in China.

The Boys School moved to new, larger premises on the south bank of the Yangtze in 1905, where the school remains to this day. The school building was designed by Alfred Davidson, who also bought the materials and hired and supervised the workmen. It was a western-looking brick building with two stories, an attic, and a little square cupola with curving eaves as a gesture to its Chinese setting. There were classrooms, teachers' bedrooms and dormitories for forty boys.

A hundred feet above the school there was a large verandahed house for the Headmaster. The formal opening ceremony took place on 10 June 1905 in the presence of the British Consul, the German Consul and a representative of the Taotai (local government). Senior pupils gave demonstrations of trigonometry, chemistry, and English recitation, and in the afternoon there was a gymnastics display. The boys concluded with "three English cheers" for the Emperor, the King of England, and the Consuls.[xcv]

By 1906, the school had grown to 65 boys, and was drawing pupils from hundreds of miles away, including one from another province. The school charged a fee of 30 silver taels per annum, which put it out of reach of most Chinese Christians, though there were some scholarships available. And although, as a Christian school, it had compulsory religious education, many of the boys came from a class traditionally hostile to Christianity, and were there only for the western education offered. Perhaps 80% of them were still non-Christians when they left, and would sometimes celebrate their graduation by tearing up their Bibles in the classroom.

What brought Alfred Davidson closest to his pupils, and one of his greatest achievements in Chungking, was sport. He was passionate about many sports – tennis, cricket, athletics – but most of all football.

After building the Boys School at Wen Feng Ta, he immediately excavated and levelled an area in front of it to use as a sports ground. To the end of his life his proudest boast was this making of a flat space in the hilly Sichuan landscape.

The Quaker China Committee back in London were not impressed: *"we regret extremely that Alfred Davidson should have gone out of his way to spend GBP 39 on a playground for the boys not originally estimated for...".* But few things contributed more to the development of the school.

Here Alfred trained the first football team in western China, the Chungking Foxes. They were named after an amateur Quaker team in London and wore European football clothes, in sharp contrast to their Chinese pigtails.

Each class at the school had one hour of football training per day, starting with basic skills like running and shooting at goal. Once the Chungking Foxes were trained, the problem was finding opponents.

Alfred thought of the British gunboat crews who were stationed in Chungking at that time to protect British interests in the newly opened treaty port. They eagerly welcomed the break from the tedium of their patrols and the playing fields of Wen Feng Ta became a place where British Seamen and Chinese literati met on equal terms, bridging as wide a cultural gap as one can imagine.

These matches became a tradition which lasted for decades, providing a point of friendly contact even during times of acute tension between the two countries.

On one memorable occasion, the Chungking Foxes beat the visiting British gunboat team. As compensation, the gunboat crew awarded the school an iron bell from the ship's mast as a reward. The bell remains at the Friends High School to this day, and is used everyday to signal the start and end of class.

In 2010, to mark the 10th anniversary of the latest incarnation of the British Consulate in Chungking, a British Consulate and British expat community team played against the school in an anniversary match. An 88-year-old local and former member of the Chungking Foxes team under Alfred Davidson attended the match and blew the starting whistle.

Football match between British Consulate-General Chongqing staff and Friends High School students as part of series of events to mark the 10th anniversary of the British Consulate-General Chongqing in 2010

Friends Boys School physical education class (Source: http://www.quaker.org.uk/files/13-93.al4boysschooldrill(1898).jpg)

Football was the game for which Friends High School became famous, but in the early days there was also cricket. Old photographs show boys kitted out in cricket whites on the school play fields high above the city. A fibre mat was laid on the stony ground to make play easier. But with most other missionary schools having North American roots, the school suffered from a lack of competition in cricket and the sport was eventually replaced by basketball.

Athletics was also introduced. On 3 April 1906 the Wen Feng Ta sports ground saw the first athletics competition ever held in Chungking. All the mission schools in the city sent teams and about two thousand people climbed the hill to watch. There were track races, long and high jumps, sack and three-legged races, and tugs-of-war. The British Consul acted as referee and awarded prizes to the winners. The event was so successful it became an annual one.

The wind of change blowing through the Chinese education system at the time also placed more emphasis on physical fitness. By 1909, the Quakers felt that the time had come to invite government schools to send teams to the annual sports day. The enlarged sports day on 4 May 1909 was a great success. 10,000 people attended and the boatmen on the river had one of the busiest days of their lives, ferrying passengers between banks. *"It is not too much to say,"* wrote Warburton, *"that the whole city of 500,000 people was centred, for that day at any rate, on the Friends' School"*. The grounds were decorated with flags, and each school's team marched under its own banner and dressed in its own uniform.

Throughout the period described in this book, there were periodic attacks on foreigners in western China, both by the soldiers of local warlords and locals angry at China's treatment at the hands of imperialist western powers.

Foreigners in general learnt to live with these periodic bouts of violence, which sometimes required them, by order of the Consul, to take refuge on the nearest British warship stationed on the Yangtze.

But by the early 1920s fighting between rival warlords was becoming more frequent and detrimental to everyday life in the region, reflecting the political backdrop of the times. Missionaries were increasingly the target of anti-foreigner feeling. They were frequently attacked, verbally abused and their properties ransacked and robbed. *"So bad is it"*, wrote Warburton, *"that it is a veritable miracle, as great as any recorded in the New Testament, for a man to be a real Christian in Chungking.*[xcvi]

In the 1920s, after nearly forty years of Protestant missionary work in the city, there were little over 1000 adherents to show for it; and in 1912 a Canadian missionary estimated that only about twenty of these led what he called "really good lives".

Armies succeeded each other with alarming rapidity. In 1923 alone, Chungking changed hands five times, and the city paid out over 5 million dollars to its various occupiers.

There were approximately 150 foreigners in Chungking in 1922, the majority of them missionaries and their families. Anti-Christian feeling was stronger than it had been at any time since the 19th century. By the end of 1923 the Foreign Office had taken the step of asking all missionary societies not to send any more recruits to Western China because of the dangerous conditions there.

Throughout this period, bandits terrorised the nearby countryside, robbing farmhouses and capturing rich people for ransom. The nights were often broken by gunfire and yelling, and bodies would be found on the roads in the morning. An army of Guizhou troops of uncertain and shifting allegiances set up its headquarters just outside the gates of the Quaker Boys School in 1924, then occupied the south bank of the river and prevented anyone from crossing. This happened at least four times between July and October of that year.

Everywhere coolies were press-ganged into service. In the city it was the water-carriers who suffered, and the price of a bucket of water soared. Grace Service reports: "instead of paying 40 cash for a man's load (two large pailfuls), we had to pay 300 cash or more – and even then sometimes we could not get enough to do our laundry."xcvii

In the countryside so many men had been press-ganged by the army that chair-bearers became extortionate. People everywhere were scared. All able-bodied men kept out of sight, those working in fields fled at the sight of a passerby, in case they were soldiers. Entering a town at nightfall was like *"entering a place of the dead: no lights, no people"*.

Grace Service records that by the end of 1923: *"soldiers were everywhere on the hills, and trouble was in the air. In fact, we were in the midst of war. Chungking was besieged by an erstwhile robber chief who used to be an ally of General Yang Sen. Now he had turned traitor and was taking advantage of General Yang's absence. His forces occupied the south bank of the Yangtze ("our side" with its hills and summer bungalows), and began to fire cannons at the city across the river."xcviii*

Institutes such as that of the Quakers and the YMCA slowly began to fall into decline as foreigners were advised to leave Sichuan. Some missionaries returned in the later 1920s and early 1930s when conditions had quietened down, but the foreign community had shrivelled by then and there were simply not even of them to sustain the kind of social activities described above.

At times foreign buildings suffered direct gunfire. Quaker Robert Warburton and his wife Pearl record taking refuge in a brick stairwell of their house while bullets peppered the house. Soldiers with artillery also occupied the school hall and dining room at times. It was impossible to walk down the road without having insults shouted at you.

In the autumn of 1924 the ruler of Chungking was a General Chao, known as the Butcher from the number of executions he ordered. Decapitations, sometimes prolonged and bloody, watched by laughing, jeering crowds of all ages, were common.

The streets of Chungking were plastered with anti-British slogans and foreigners took refuge in the foreign-owned *godowns* on the south bank. Foreign bungalows on the hills were looted and smashed up, the paths strewn with broken gramophone records and sewing machines. Sometimes the very structure of the buildings was taken apart for the valuable wood and glass in them.

By 1926 there were only 2 British residents left in the foreign community on the south bank of the Yangtze – Alfred Davidson and Irene Hutchinson – and this did not go unnoticed by locals. The following week they heard that an "Anti-Humiliation Society" in the city was talking of capturing them and exhibiting them in cages. Placards went up offering $100 reward for the head of an Englishman.[xcix] The few remaining British businesses in the city were being boycotted.

Banditry on the Yangtze also grew as the increase in steamer traffic threw thousands of junkmen and trackers out of work, and they had little choice but to join the disbanded soldiers and professional robbers already busy fleecing travellers.[c]

By 1930 there were said to be more soldiers in Chungking than in the whole of the British army.

By this time there were only 3 British Quakers left in the whole of Szechwan province. The Friends school in Chungking had begun to suffer from the climate of the times.

"Most of these boys," writes Alfred Davidson, *"come from homes where the father thinks it the height of happiness to have three or four wives"*. The school had three years to try and inculcate different values, yet every holiday the boys would return to their polygamous, opium-smoking homes and at the end of the three years *"they leave us to drop back into the sink of uncleanness...I could fill pages with the wrecks our old boys have made of their lives."*[ci]

Western China was now so backward and corrupt that it was difficult for the boys to find any decent employment when they left. The ambition of most of them was to work for the Post Office or for foreign businesses, but army life proved an overwhelming temptation for many.

Into the 1930s, hostility to foreigners remained high, even though the mass movements and fierce nationalism of the 1920s had died down. Alfred Davidson comments: *"I never leave the school grounds but I am cursed up hill and down dale by all sorts and conditions of people. I try to be indifferent to it, but at times when the language is particularly filthy I find it very difficult to keep quiet. To live in this atmosphere of antagonism all the time is very trying to one's nerves and temper, and one longs for quiet, the sense of security and the friendliness of home."*[cii]

The Mayor of Chungking, hearing of the murder of British missionary Clifford Stubbs around this time is said to have remarked, *"It would have been better if there had been a few more."*

Sichuan, as much of the rest of China, was descending deeper into abject poverty and a feeling of fear and despair reigned. Unemployment and starvation were rife: Alfred Davidson remarked that he had never seen so many beggars in the streets and so many coffins being carried up from the river to the burial mounds on the hills. Often bodies were just dumped by the roadside and left unburied.

Now too old for regular sport, Davidson kept himself busy by tending to a small vegetable plot on the hillside near the school, but as soon as the vegetables were ready to eat, they were invariably stolen. He commented; *"Hope springs eternal in the human beat, even where cauliflowers are concerned and one is surrounded by starving Chinese."*[ciii]

Lawlessness ruled in the city and the few remaining missionaries left on the hillside took to ruling over their own little kingdom, sitting in judgement of thieves and trespassers and usually dismissing them with a hot meal or suit of clothes. Old China had resolutely died and all the traditional moral values of old Chinese society had disappeared to leave hopelessness and apathy in their wake. People were living in a kind of limbo, waiting for a new, better society to come along, but incapable of bringing that about.

The Kuomintang brought to Sichuan a militaristic nationalism which placed Quakers schools in particular in great difficulty. The government introduced flag raising ceremonies in the morning and afternoon where pupils had to stand to attention.

Military training also became compulsory for all Senior Middle School students. The pacifist Quakers refused to introduce this and applied for an exemption, which they were refused. They were forced to close down the senior class in 1937, but by then there were few boys in the class anyway: when the whole country was overcome by military fervour and drilling, young boys hated to be excluded and were leaving for other schools. Other missionary schools embraced the military drill with enthusiasm, eager to show themselves patriotic.

Writing in 1935, Alfred Davidson lamented:

"As I have got older, my faith has become very precious to me, many a time I get down in the dumps and feel utterly miserable at being separated from all those I love best in the world, and at such times there is no one to turn to but the God we know in Jesus, and if I could not turn to him and pour out my hear to Him I don't know what I should do.... It is this faith that has kept me going all these years alone in this land of dirt, civil war and utter misery." [civ]

The Quaker Boys School finally closed down in 1937 and Alfred Davidson left China for the last time, having spent 53 years of his life in the city.

Three days earlier thieves had broken into his house as he slept and took clothes, blankets, shoes and suitcases packed ready for his planned home leave. Before leaving they even took chicken from the meat safe and ate it on the balcony. It was the third robbery he had suffered in as many years: China, it seemed, was determined to show him its worse face right up until the end.

By 1949 and the Communist Revolution, China closed its doors to the outside world. Most foreign missionaries that remained in the country were forced to pack up and leave – those that remained risked their lives.

A Foreign Office report from 1951 details how *"Directives from Peking to provincial authorities pointing out that all foreign missionaries are tainted with "imperialism" and potential spies requiring watching were issued in the autumn last year. Since then a number have been arrested.. At the present time, almost thirty or so of them are in gaol (almost all of them being American or Canadian) which is probably more than at any time since the anti-foreigner period of the Boxer rebellion (1900). There have been several occasions of public trials, confessions &c. Charges are frequently not proffered. Access to persons so arrested is usually denied. A typical case is that of Dr Stewart Allen, in charge of the Canadian Missionary Hospital in Chungking (formerly our Embassy Doctor), a devoted and highly competent medical man and highly respected by the Chinese. He was arrested in December, accused of a "reactionary" attitude. The Chinese press reported inter alia that he had poisoned progressive minded patients. A number of missionary schools, universities and hospitals have been taken over".[cv]*

Those that chose to remain included William Sewell - one of the few foreign teachers invited to stay in China during the early 1950s. He continued his teaching at the West China Union University in Chengdu, returning to England in 1952. He and others tried to adapt to the times, living simply and sharing with others.

The Communist Government had, in early 1950, told all missionaries that we could no longer pass out tracts or literature of any kind. All youth work was forbidden, as the government decreed the youth were too busy with other more important activities. All church meetings had to be registered with the government, and no group meetings could be held without the permission of the government. One Sunday, the afternoon English Worship Service for English Speaking People was interrupted and closed because someone had failed to get the required permit.

The propaganda and slogans of the government were very profuse. Some often-seen slogans were: "Down with

Imperialism," "Down with Capitalism," "Down with America," "Imperialistic Americans buy the favour of the people with money," and "People are paid to attend Church." In the rural areas, a popular saying was, "Down with the Land-Lords." Many Landlords, in fact, were arrested because of the high rents that they had charged the poor renters during the past years.

Those that wanted to leave China, had to register to do so, then wait several months before their name was chosen, when they would have to prepare to leave within hours of being informed. This marked the definitive end of the myth of western China as a hidden El Dorado.

The work of the Friends Mission carried on for some time after that, in the hands of Yang Fang-ling, the Davidson's trusted partner. But he suffered at the hands of the Red Guards in 1951, denounced on grounds that he betrayed left-wing students at the school to Chiang Kai-Shek's secret police, who tortured them to death.[cvi] It seems it was a member of his own teaching staff that denounced him. His property was confiscated, he was sent to prison for life and his family was labelled as "enemies of the people". He died in prison in 1960.

By 1959 and the start of the Cultural Revolution, all churches were closed, religious practice was forbidden and Christians emprisoned. Anyone with foreign connections was in danger and all records of the past, including church archives, family papers and photographs were destroyed, often by the owners themselves.

The old school building at Wen Feng Ta was destroyed by Red Guards too, but the master's house above the school, where the Davidsons had lived, remains to this day.

A new Friends school has arisen on the same site, which now wears its British history with pride, including old photographs from the Davidson times on the walls in its corridors. It still excels in sports and has maintained the sports field and athletics track that the Davidsons built them almost one hundred years before.

The impact that missionaries ultimately had in western China in religious terms was minimal. There were probably twenty times more Muslims than Christians in China in 1900. Christians never comprised more than one percent of Chinese, which the Boxer rising reduced by the subtraction of some 30,000 martyrs. Moreover, the majority of Chinese Christians were Catholic, amounting to perhaps one-and-a-half million in the whole of China by 1914. Protestants, by contrast, numbered perhaps just 190,000.[cvii]

It is on the social and cultural life of cities such as Chungking in western China that the missionaries' effect was more profound. Churches and schools from this period survive amongst the modern fabric of cities such as Chungking and Chengdu today. There are also fine examples in remote provincial towns such as x... In some cases, churches have been moved brick by brick from one location to another to make way for modern infrastructure developments, but are preserved for their historical value, and through a growing recognition by the Communist authorities that religion, if closely monitored, has an important role to play in promoting social cohesion and higher values.

But missionaries were not just preachers of the Christian gospel and founders of churches. They were, for a time, the main mediators of western civilisation to a society which felt an urgent need for it, but was equally repulsed and fascinated by it. This was particularly true in western China where for many decades missionaries were almost the only representatives of the west.

Missionaries oversaw the introduction of western educational methods, and as we will see in a later chapter, western science and geography, photography and printing methods. They brought western medicine and western sports. The hygiene campaigns run by the YMCA and the Chungking institute anticipated the great nationwide campaigns of the new government in the 1950s.

Chapter 6:

<u>Science</u>

"The greatest service which can be rendered to any country is to add a useful plant to its culture"

Thomas Jefferson

It is well-known that China has produced more scientific inventions than any other civilisation: printing, gunpowder, the compass, paper, and so on.

But this may not have been immediately obvious in the China of the 19th century. China had fallen way behind the West in terms of scientific development by this time, and remained in many ways in a medieval time warp. When westerners arrived with their steamships, trains, modern materials and techniques, it proved quite a shock to the local population and incited much interest.

China was at a crossroads in the late 19th and early 20th centuries. As Edwin Dingle writes:

"The Chinese…of interior provinces such as Szech-wan… are realizing that they hold an obscure position. I have heard educated Chinese remark that they look upon themselves as lost, like shipwrecked sailors, whom a night of tempest has cast on some lonely rock; and now they are having recourse to cries, volleys, all the signals imaginable, to let it be known that they are still there. They have been on this lonely isolated rock as far as history can trace. Now they are launching out towards progress, towards the making of things, towards the buying and selling of things--launching out in trade and in commerce, in politics, in literature, in science, in all that has spelt advance in the West. The modern spirit is spreading speedily into the domains of life everywhere--in places swiftly, in places slowly, but spreading inevitably."[cviii] This chapter looks at the influence of British scientific invention and ingenuity on western China and the lasting influence of British and Chinese scientific contact.

Any discussion of science and China must start with Joseph Needham – no relation, by the way.

Needham, a sinologist at Cambridge University, was sent to China in 1943 to assume the role of Head of the Sino-British Scientific Co-operation Office, which was officially attached to the British Embassy in wartime Chungking. His specific role was "to do everything in my power to renew and extend the cultural bonds between the British and Chinese peoples", including helping to create links between new China's universities and the UK, and through doing so, to help in the rebuilding of war torn China through the education of its most talented.

The British Science Office became the predecessor of the British Council in China, which continues to work across the work with similar aims, including in present day Chongqing.

Needham was chosen for the role given his long-standing interest in China and the Chinese language, and his scientific background. In the mid 1930s Needham had met three young Chinese researchers who had come to work at the University of Cambridge. The interest these bright young people aroused moved him to begin learning Chinese and gain a deeper knowledge of Chinese culture. And what he began to learn astonished him.

Needham took up offices on the British Embassy compound - a ramshackle agglomeration of long, narrow buildings on a bewildering variety of levels on a steeply terraced hillside on the right bank of the Yangtze. The buildings were connected to each other by a network of steep staircases running through the woods which had a cheap, temporary look, all lath and plaster with bamboo sunshades.

Everything was dilapidated, plaster had fallen off several walls, exposing the bamboo matting underneath, and some of the buildings leaned alarmingly, especially those perched at the top of the fast-eroding slopes that crumbled down the riverbank[cix].

Needham records his first impressions of Chungking as follows:

"It is an extremely sprawling place, running along at different levels for several miles so that there is plenty of green about everywhere, and the sound of cocks and hens even in the midst of the city. Hence there is a certain resemblance to Torquay, which the red-dish earth and some of the masonry makes you think of, but the hills are higher... At night, when the lights are out, and you hear the sirens of the river steamers (an ever-present sound, though not so frequent as in New York), the place is said to resemble Hong Kong. It also resembles Harpers Ferry, where the Shenandoah joins the Potomac, and the sirens of the B&O trains redound.. but the scenery is on a larger scale here. It seems that the city contains nothing old and beautiful architecturally, but rather masses of jerrybuilt structures put up after the bombings had destroyed everything that was there before."[cx]

Needham travelled around Western China visiting its universities and providing them above all with the supplies they needed to kick-start their research potential again: laboratory equipment, reference books, scientific journals.

He was given permission to bring in supplies via the air bridge over the Hump – the only feasible route into western China during the Second World War – all transportation costs to be borne by the British government.

Needham was allotted space on the inbound flights and an acceptable tonnage at least once a week, for a generous number of boxes which would be assembled in Calcutta on the basis of his requests. These included copies of Nature for a physicist in Chungking, scalpels and a dissecting table for a biologist in Chengdu, and a list of poisonous plants of the Shan states for the geologists at the Chinese survey.

But perhaps most important for history is the private work Needham accomplished while travelling across China on his official duties.

Needham was fascinated by the history of Chinese science – that China had been a hotbed of the vast majority of scientific discoveries over the preceding centuries. It became clear to him, for instance, that printing, the magnetic compass and gunpowder weapons were all Chinese in origin,

The importance with which early modern western society judged these technologies was clearly expressed by Francis Bacon as early as 1620 when he wrote:

"Printing, gunpowder and the compass ... whence have followed innumerable changes, in so much that no empire, no sect, no star seems to have exerted greater power and influence in human affairs than these mechanical discoveries."

Bacon was likely unaware when he wrote this of the origins of these inventions, and was not writing of the ancient Chinese inventions but rather their Western analogs.

Needham set out to write a history of Chinese science – in the process making discoveries about China that very few Chinese of the time even knew. An example of one of Needham's unexpected discoveries occurred in the remote Sichuanese town of Lizhuang where Needham discovered an Institute of History – an outpost of the Academia Sinica, an organisation much like the UK's Royal Society – which was filled with the most unexpected treasures. Needham's diary for 10 June 1943 reads:

"You wouldn't believe the treasures they have there. The archaeological section has plenty of Han-time bronzes and jade objects, but the marvel is the famous oracle bones of Shang time from the tombs oat Anyang (1300 – 1100 BC) which have the most ancient writing on them.

The people here are running out of tissue paper on which to make their rubbings, so I shall try to get some from India for them. Then the Historical section has lots of bamboo tablets on which the Classics were written in Confucius' time, and also marvellous Imperial Archives from the early Qing dynasty, including letters to the Jesuits and decrees to Tibet and a document from the Chinese court appointing the Japanese shogun as King of that country.

The Linguistic section has gramophone records of the dialects of every province. And so on, and so on. The libraries are wonderful.... Authentic specimens of Song dynasty movable block printed books and the like.."

During the course of this visit Needham came across a decree forbidding the sale of gunpowder to the Tartars in AD 1076, leading him to conclude that the Chinese had discovered gunpowder a full two centuries before Berthold Schwarz's alleged discovery in the west.[cxi] It was a similar story in many other places Needham visited.

Amongst the long list of discoveries Needham attributed to China were the abacus, anti-malaria drugs, the air conditioning fan, ball bearings, bookworm repellent, cast iron, coinage, the crossbow, fumigation, the kite, negative numbers in mathematics, toilet paper, an accurate estimation of Pi, playing cards, refraction, the seismograph, inoculation against smallpox, stirrups, the toothbrush and the weather vane.

As Needham concluded, *"the mere fact of seeing them listed brings home to one the astonishing inventiveness of the Chinese people."*[cxii]

The list illustrated the sheer creative fervour within Chinese society. Needham pointed out that in every century the Chinese dreamed up nearly 15 new scientific ideas – a pace of inventiveness unmatched by the world's other great ancient civilizations, including the Greeks. The nature of the invention was remarkable enough, Needham wrote; but the rate at which they came was like nowhere else on earth, and like no other time in history.[cxiii]

The resulting work, Needham's "Science and Civilization in China", remains the longest book ever written about China in the English language and a reference for the history of Chinese science.

From the first volume published in 1954, the work had swollen to 18 volumes by the time Needham died in 1995. It now runs to 24 volumes as dedicated researchers at the Needham Institute in Cambridge continue to take forward the project, which remains to this day incomplete. As the project has broadened, so has the range of questions under investigation. It is widely acknowledged to be the greatest work of explanation of the Middle Kingdom yet to be created in western history.

Through the writing of the work, Needham became enthralled by one question in particular, which came to be known as the "Needham question": after such a rich history of scientific invention, why did China suddenly stop inventing things around the middle of the 15th century, leading Europe to take the lead role in advancing the world's civilisation? Why was China unable to hold on to its early advantage and creative edge? Why, by the 18th and 19th centuries, was China a nation known principally for being backward, hostile, and poor?

Needham looked at various explanations in turn – geographical, social, economic, bureaucratic, linguistic. Did China's reliance on an ideographic system of writing inhibit the development of Chinese science? Did bureaucracy play a role?

Needham never fully worked out the answer in his lifetime, and it is one sinologists continue to debate even today. Some point to the homogenous nature and isolation of the Chinese state. Europe by contrast was packed with the competing ambitions of numerous states. If one needed to produce a better cannon than another, its technologists would be cajoled into trying to do so, leading to healthy competition. Plenty of technology existed outside China but there was little need for China to compete, so no driving pressure for improvement over the centuries.

It is now clear that no simple answer to Needham's original question will be possible. The quest has opened out into an investigation of the ways in which scientific and technical activity have been linked with the development of Chinese society over the last four millennia. Even so, Needham's work represents a remarkable body of knowledge about China and its scientific development and remains to this day a reference. China itself has recognized Needham's contribution to extending knowledge about the country and its scientific achievements. Needham remains widely known there under his Chinese name of Li Yue-se.

By the time Needham left China in 1947 he had visited a total of 296 universities, institutes and research establishments; he had arranged for the delivery of thousands of tons of equipment and chemical and scientific journals; he had collected a body of thousands of documents in order to enhance his and others' knowledge of China; and he spent much of his final months laying the foundations for a diplomatically privileged organisation to support Chinese science - an organisation – the British Council – that would continue to function long after Needham had left.[cxiv]

At the end of World War II, Needham was invited to take part in the founding of a new organization under the auspices of the United Nations which would promote world peace through scientific and cultural co-operation, UNESCO. In fact, had it not been for Needham's insistence on including science within the organisation's remit, that organization might be known today under the title UNECO.

Some viewed the aims of UNESCO with deep suspicion, assuming it was really a cover for espionage. Needham's idea of placing scientific field offices around the world, modelled on the Scientific Co-operation Office he led in Chungking was to more paranoid minds, no more than a thinly veiled means of putting spies in place under deep cover.[cxv] The Americans were the most suspicious and went as far of accusing UNESCO of being infiltrated by communists, naming Needham in the process.

Within a month President Truman's administration had placed numerous bureaucratic hurdles in Needham's way, and flatly refused to hand out money to any scientific unions that Washington deemed left wing. After just two years with UNESCO Needham promptly resigned, relived to be getting back to his studies and away from the feuding that characterized this particular period of the Cold War.

Needham went on to found and become the first President of the Britain - China Friendship Society in 1955 – a way of underlining his support for Mao and Mao's regime in Communist China. The organisation was a briefly powerful and always controversial group. Its 2000 strong membership at the time saw itself as essential bridge-builders: criticising Britain's lukewarm policy towards Communist China, lobbying for an increase in trade and arguing the case for China's membership of the United Nations. The organisation continues to exist to this day promoting friendship and understanding between the two countries.

Needham then went on to found the Society for Anglo-Chinese understanding (SACU), which became one of few means through which the British were able to visit China during the dark years of the 1950s and 1960s. The young David Attenborough was one of the first to do so through this channel. Needham remained the President of SACU for 35 years, visiting China frequently during the years of the Great Leap Forward and Cultural Revolution, dismayed by what he saw, but still retaining a passion for all things Chinese.

Needham died in 1992 but the Needham Institute at Cambridge University remains a centre for excellence in East Asian science, technology and medicine, with strong links to China.

Yangtze River explorer

Britons played an important role in mapping the Yangtze river and expanding western knowledge of the river basin and its natural assets. In order to gain access deep into western China, it was first necessary to accurately map the physical landscape and the challenges and obstacles it contained.

Britons had the technical know-how to do this, and cartographers and navigators were dispatched from the mid 1850s onwards to explorer the upper reaches of the Yangtze river basin, amongst them Thomas Blakiston, William Gill and Cornell Plant.

These men were encouraged in their endeavours by British merchants who dreamt of the untold riches, of the mineral wealth, and of the crops, plants and flowers of inland China – all ripe for discovery by the intrepid adventurer.

The early success of the sale of opium to the Chinese in exchange for tea had proved the possibilities of the trade in nature's riches. The opium-for-tea exchange was indispensable to Great Britain. Nearly one in every ten pounds sterling collected by the government came from the import and sale of tea – about a pound per person per year.

Tea taxes funded railways, roads and Civil Service salaries, essential to an emerging industrial economy. Opium was equally significant to the British economy for it financed the management of India – the shining jewel in Queen Victoria's imperial crown.

As flowers swelled the balance sheets of the Oriental trade, the men who understood them – men once called gardeners – were now regarded as members of a new profession: botany. The emergent botanists became swashbucklers and world changers in their own right, scouring the Empire in search of the new and exotic.

Foreign plants were collected and studied for the potential scientific, economic and agricultural advances they might offer, with the added benefit of a little western know-how.[cxvi] There was also an interest in the minority peoples who inhabited many of these remote extremities of the Chinese Empire and the knowledge that they possessed in terms of exploiting and caring for the natural assets of their region.

The earliest of the British explorers of the upper Yangtze river was Thomas Blakiston (1832-91), an army officer, explorer and naturalist. Blakiston was one of the very first foreigners to travel through the treacherous Three Gorges.

In 1850s he spent 5 months travelling up the Yangtze River, going a distance of 1800 miles, further than any Westerner before him. He surveyed the course of the river to such a high standard that his charts were still in use well into the 1920s.

The book he wrote about the journey, *Five Months on the Yang-tze*, remained the stand navigational text for the river well into the twentieth century. He is also noted for his meticulous and elegant writings on the birds and plants of

Sichuan, and descriptions of the political turmoil in the China he saw, during the Taiping Rebelion.

In 1860 Blakiston was awarded the Royal Geographical Society Medal for his work on the Yangtze, an honour he shared that year with Thomas Wills, one of the explorers who mapped the interior of Australia.

William Gill was another early explorer of the West. A member of the Royal Engineers by profession, Gill was fortunate enough to inherit a small fortune at a young age, and as well as his army duties combined his career with his passion for journeys of exploration, at the same time gathering intelligence for the British government.

Early in May 1876, William Gill was wondering where next to explore. A friend he met in Trafalgar Square suggested China and within a fortnight Gill had been convinced of the idea, helped by advice from family friend Baron von Richthofen, himself a seasoned explorer of western China.

Gill travelled around the headwaters of the Yangtze in the extreme west of China, mapping the elevations of the area and chronicling the wide variety of minority peoples that lived there.

William Gill's scientific work, including the Chinese expeditions, was recognised in 1879 when the Royal Geographical Society (RGS) awarded him one of its two annual gold medals. The RGS award cited in particular *'the careful series of hypsometrical observations and the traverse survey' made in western China and Tibet, 'by which we have for the first time, the means of constructing with considerable accuracy profile sections of those elevated and little known regions.'*

Not only had he conducted valuable survey work but he had also brought back much interesting information about the tribes he encountered. These included the Musus and the Lisus, whose women wore costumes similar to the traditional Swiss style. Moreover, from the Musus he brought back to the British Museum a remarkable manuscript. This was in an unknown script, which an expert of the time thought might be a survival of a very ancient ideographic system, a way of depicting ideas via symbols.

The following year, the Geographical Society of Paris awarded William Gill a gold medal and John Murray published Gill's two-volume account of the journey entitled *The River of Golden Sand, the narrative of a journey through China and Eastern Tibet to Burmah.* Baron von Richtofen was deeply impressed by William Gill's work and has described him as *"an acute observer of men and nature, [who] stands very high indeed by the accuracy and persistency with which he has carried through his surveying work ... Many a famous traveller might learn in this respect from Captain Gill. The determination of so many altitudes is too a very important part of his work ..."*[cxvii]

Cornell Plant

Cartographer and navigator Cornell Plant (Pu Lan Tian in Chinese) is recorded in history as the man who mapped the Yangtze river – at that time, considered one of the most dangerous rivers in the world the Yangtze.

Plant spent much of his working life in China fulfilling this task, at a time when the Chinese laughed at the misguided madness of the British who thought they could succeed in taking a powered vessel through the whirlpools and rapids of the Three Gorges.

Indeed Cornell Plant's story is intimately linked to those efforts to make the first ascension of the Yangtze River by steamship, through a chance association with Archibald Little, mentioned earlier in this book - another celebrated Briton in the history of Britain's association with western China.

Plant met Archibald Little in the Oriental Club in London in 1899, where Little was meeting potential investors to drum up funds for the attempt to navigate the Three Gorges by steamship. The meeting proved important for both men.

Archibald Little was back in the UK to supervise the building of a paddle steamer designed for the task. He needed an experienced and professional river pilot to command it. Cornell Plant needed just such employment.

He must have been enthralled by Little's description of the great Yangtze river, its problems and its dangers. The undoubted difficulties that Plant had overcome on the Karun River in modern day Iran were trivial in comparison with the many natural hazards that existed in the Upper Yangtze, where the annual snow melt in the high mountains and the seasonal rainfall combined to produce variations in the height of water of as much as 150 feet - a scarcely believable phenomenon to a deep sea sailor. Plant was used to rocks, rapids and river water turbulence, but not the standing whirlpools, the moving whirlpools, the sudden holes that appeared in deep water and the rapidly changing nature of the river bed.

The talk must have whetted his professional appetite to such an extent that he even joined Little on his trip to Denny's of Glasgow where the new paddle steamer, the *Pioneer* was being built, then shipped to Shanghai in kit form to be assembled there. The result of their meeting was that Cornell Plant joined Archibald Little in China and took command of the *Pioneer* on her voyage up through the gorges, the first truly successful trip by a commercial vessel driven by steam.

Even earlier British explorers such as Blakiston had warned against the dangers of attempting an ascent of the Three Gorges by steam vessel, judging it an impossible task. However Plant succeeded, making the journey in the Pioneer from Yichang to Chungking in just 73 steaming hours spread over 7 days total. This was because one rapid held up the voyage for three whole nerve-racking days.

Later the Royal Navy commandeered the Pioneer for its own uses and changed its named to the HMS Kinsha. She was used for over 20 years to patrol the Yangtze and evacuate British civilians caught up in outbreaks of trouble along the Yangtze.

Later Plant bought himself a houseboat junk and used this to trade up and down the river between Ichang and Chungking, all the while studying the river and its treacherous rapids. He soon gained the deep respect of ail the junkmen he came into contact with for his knowledge of the river.

Several years later Plant was approached by the Chinese-owned Szechwan Steam Navigation Company to assist in the design of a purpose built steamer to trade on the Upper Yangtze. This vessel "Shunting" was built in Southampton by Thorneycrofts for £6, 000. She was 115 feet long, 16 feet beam and drew 3 feet. Under Plant's command the Shutting operated a 14-day service between Ichang and Chungking. She carried 12 first class passengers, 66 deck passengers and 60 tons of cargo in lighters lashed alongside the vessel. The service proved to be very popular and a second vessel the Shilling was commissioned.

In 1910 Plant was offered the post of Senior Inspector, Upper Yangtze in the Imperial Maritime Customs Service – a prestigious body set up under the Treaty of Nanking which allowed foreigners, particularly the British, to collect customs duties on behalf of the Chinese government. It enabled the British to exert a huge economic and political influence on the Chinese government, and its men contributed hugely to the advancement of knowledge of every obscure corner of the Chinese Empire through the Service's meticulously researched trade reports.

Plant's particular contribution to this body of knowledge was a publication, 'Handbook for the Guidance of Shipmasters on the Ichang-Chungking Section of the Yangtze River.' In its 80 pages Plant examines with painstaking precision every rock and cliff, rapid and whirlpool, and twist and turn of the Yangtze River. He gave names to rocks and whirlpools which had none, and gathered the Chinese names of others through his contacts with local junkmen. He also recorded many legends of the river in his crib sheets. It became an essential part of a navigator's kit, showing captains in numbered diagrams (for non-English readers) how to approach a rapid and follow the axis of its current, and – crucially - how to back out of the white-water maelstrom if things started to go awry.

The book could be found on the bridges of ships and junks for more than half a century, its pages dog-eared and marked with pencil by many a nervous but grateful skipper. The series of signal stations Plant set up along the river to aid navigation are still very much in use today.

Plant retired from the Imperial Maritime Customs Service in 1919. In recognition of his outstanding service, the Service and the Chinese Government built him a small bungalow on the outskirts of the village of Xintang, where he chose to live out his remaining days. This bungalow perched on a small promontory overlooking the mouth of the Xiling Gorge and the Hsin T'an Rapids. Steamers using this stretch of the river saluted Captain Plant by sounding their whistles and he would reply by waving his hat or handkerchief.[cxviii]

In 1921, the Plants decided to visit England for a holiday before returning to Xintan to live out the rest of their lives. In Shanghai, they boarded the Blue Funnel line's SS Teiresias, which was to take them to Europe via various ports.

En route to Hong Kong, however, Plant, aged 54, came down with pneumonia. He died at sea on February 26, 1921. Tragedy struck again when Plant's wife Alice also passed away - just two days after the ship docked in Victoria Harbour, Hong Kong. She, too, died of pneumonia, but perhaps pining for her lifelong companion exacerbated her condition.

They were buried together in Happy Valley Cemetery in Hong Kong, where the inscription on their tomb reads: 'In memory of Captain Samuel Cornell Plant; Upper Yangtze River Inspector of the Chinese Maritime Customs. The first to command a merchant steamer plying on the Upper Yangtze River (1900). Also in Memory of Alice Sophia Plant, Captain Plant's wife and devoted companion throughout his 20 years of toil on the dangerous section of the Yangtze

River between Ichang and Chungking.'

Plant is one of very few foreigners whose lives are commemorated in China with monuments.

A 30-foot obelisk in the village of Xintang, where the Dragon Horse Stream flows into the Yangtze, remembers his unique contribution to navigation on the formidable Yangtze river. The British Consulate in Chungking collected subscriptions from expatriates and other interested people to raise the memorial. The inscription, which was in both English and Chinese, was eradicated by the Red Guards in 1968 after they had, unsuccessfully, tried to blow it up.

The monument has risked becoming victim to the rising waters of the Three Gorges reservoir behind the Three gorges Dam in recent years, but the writer's understanding is that the monument is still intact, although now much closer to the water's edge than it once was.

The then British Consul at Ichang. a good friend of Plant's, summed up his feelings at the loss of Plant and his wife Alice in a letter to his younger brother Charles as follows: *"Their deaths create a great gap in the Upper River community life and your brother's experience was so great and his work up here consequently so good that it is impossible to adequately replace him"*. Plant himself summed up his love of the Yangtze river as follows: *"truly, the farther one travels along this mighty water highway of China, the more strangely fascinating it becomes"*.[cxix]

These days around 1.5 billion tonnes of cargo is carried on the Yangtze River each year, making it the busiest freight waterway in the world, ahead of the Mississippi in the United States and the Rhine in Europe.

The Three Gorges Dam, which went into operation in 2006, may have deeply submerged many of the worst hazards but the authorities still use the navigation system and rules and regulations designed by Plant. His nautical marks - black triangles and balls - are dotted along the banks; his colour-coded buoys, white for the north bank and red for the south, keep the fleet on course. And his Shipmaster's Guide and charts remain the basis on which modern pilot manuals are written.

Botanists

The Victorian era was the golden era of plant collecting. There existed a desire for exploration and discovery and Victorian plant hunters were botanical adventurers who risked life and limb to bring back to Britain exotic plants from around the world.

An astonishing number of now common garden plants were introduced for the first time during this period - from roses to rhododendrons, magnolias to camellias and primulas to azaleas and clematis. In fact, it would be very hard to find a garden in the northern planting zones that does not owe a debt of gratitude to China. The concept of the English landscape garden flourished during this period as gardeners tried out new ways of displaying their newly acquired exotic plants in arboretums and woodland gardens.

Western China was a prime destination for many plant hunters given its variety of geographical zones. George Forrest, Frank Kingdon-Ward and Ernest Wilson, amongst others, played an important role not only in introducing new species to the British landscape, but also in advancing scientific knowledge of China's flora and fauna through formal classification.

Kew Gardens became the centre of botanical research for the entire world at this time: all seeds, shrubs, specimens and herbs were forwarded from the Empire's outposts to Kew's gardeners, the ultimate arbiters of horticulture.[cxx] Wealthy British industrialists also invested in collections of rare and exotic plants as a new popular pastime, just as today's entrepreneurs might invest their wealth in fine wines or art.

George Forrest (1873–1932) was a Scottish botanist, and one of the first explorers of China's then remote south-western province of Yunnan, generally regarded as the most bio-diverse province in the country. Forrest initially travelled to Australia in the hope of making his fortune panning for gold.

When he returned to Britain in 1902 he found employment as a clerk in the Herbarium at the Royal Botanic Garden, Edinburgh. His employer, Sir Isaac Balfour, recommended him to Liverpool cotton merchant Arthur Kilpin Bulley, who was sponsoring an expedition to southwestern China in search of exotic plants, particularly species of rhododendron, for which Yunnan was famous.

Forrest made his first visit to Yunnan in 1904, accompanied by seventeen other plant collectors. Around that time, foreigners had been targeted for death by the local Tibetan Buddhist lamas, during the 1905 Tibetan Rebellion. Forrest had a narrow escape, but this did not discourage him from returning to Yunnan.

Altogether Forrest made seven trips to the province, collecting samples and seeds for the Herbarium and for avid collectors willing to pay for new species to add to their collections. In total, he brought back over 31,000 plant specimens and discovered about 600 species of plants, 300 of which were rhododendrons. He also brought back camellias, magnolias, Himalayan poppies and primulas. The specific epithet *forrestii* adorns more than thirty genera.[cxxi]

Forrest was also a pioneer of methods. Unlike other collectors at the time, he extensively employed local people as collectors – a practice which continues today amongst botanists. In addition, the quality of the data he provided for each collection – altitude, habitat, plant description etc. – far exceeded that of his peers.

In 1921 Forrest was awarded the Victoria Medal by the Royal Horticultural Society for his contributions to the advancement of scientific knowledge. He was elected a Fellow of the Linnean Society in 1924 and was presented with the Veitch Memorial Medal in 1927.

Forrest died unexpectedly in Tengchong in 1932 – a town famous for its hot springs where he frequently stayed after journeying through British-held Burma. The collections he had made during this his seventh and last trip were sent back to the Royal Botanic Gardens, Edinburgh, but Forrest was buried in Yunnan.

Ernest Wilson (1876 – 1930) was an amateur British botanist. He was sent to western China by Kew Gardens to investigate the negative impact of the charcoal industry on the forests and biodiversity of Yunnan. In addition, he was financed by private entrepreneur the Veitch nursery, which specialised in new and unusual plants for the gardens of Britain's rich, to bring back hardy new plant species.

He made four expeditions to western China in the early years of the twentieth century, bringing back such plants as the Chinese Gooseberry (or Kiwi Fruit, as we now know it), the Regal Lily and the Yellow and Red Poppyworts. He also brought back the seeds of the Handkerchief Tree (Davidia Involucrata) – a plant which had been described but never previously collected.

In all, EH 'Chinese' Wilson brought us over 1,000 garden plants and around 16,000 herbarium specimens, introducing more plants to Western horticulture than any other collector. His introductions included the Beauty Bush (*Kolkwitzia amabilis*), the *'Wilson 50'* Kurume azaleas, and the magnificent King's Lily (*Lilium regale*), the collection of which very nearly cost him his life. *Sinowilsonia henryi* from central and western China and many species are named in his honour. Wilson was awarded the Veitch Memorial Medal in1906 and the Victoria Medal of Honour in 1912 for his services to the study of botany.[cxxii]

The missionaries

Missionaries also contributed significantly to the advancement of scientific knowledge in western China, bringing western life a little bit closer to the extremities of the Chinese Empire.

As early as the 16th and 17th centuries, the Jesuit missionaries had begun to introduce western science and astronomy to China. Through figures such as Italian Matteo Ricci, who introduced Western science, mathematics, astronomy, and visual arts to the imperial court, and carried on significant inter-cultural and philosophical dialogue with Chinese scholars, particularly representatives of Confucianism.

At the time of their peak influence, members of the Jesuit delegation were considered some of the emperor's most valued and trusted advisors, holding numerous prestigious posts in the imperial government.

The Jesuits made efforts to translate western mathematical and astronomical works into Chinese and aroused the interest of Chinese scholars in these sciences. They made very extensive astronomical observation and carried out the first modern cartographic work in China.

They also learned to appreciate the scientific achievements of this ancient culture and made them known in Europe. Through their correspondence European scientists first learned about Chinese science and culture. Confucius' work, for example, was translated into European languages through the agency of Jesuit scholars stationed in China.

Later, Protestant and Catholic missionaries are credited with introducing a number of new scientific methods or equipment to western China including the western printing press and the camera. Through their work missionaries also contributed to the promotion of hygiene, environmental protection and other social causes. They also created institutions where locals could attend lectures and exhibitions to gain knowledge of scientific and economic concepts.

Quaker Mary-Jane Warburton was the founding editor of the West China Missionary News, in whose pages missionaries of the region could exchange ideas and information. Initially produced in longhand, the Quakers later invested in Chungking's first Roman-type printing press, which they shipped up the Yangtze from Shanghai, and set about training three boys from the Friends school as compositors and printers.

The newspaper was published regularly until the 1940s and provides a major source of information about the region as a whole at that time, not just missionary work.

When Archibald Little successfully captained the first steamboat to Chungking in 1898, Robert Davidson recorded the event on his camera for posterity. Many of the earliest photographic records of life in Sichuan in this period come from missionary photographers.

Photography was also a skill that the missionaries could pass on to their disciples, and a way for missionaries to maintain contact with former pupils. Initially, locals were fearful of the camera, believing that taking a picture of someone equalled stealing their soul. But once over this, there was a good market for photographic products.

The Quakers helped a number of former pupils found the Chungking Photo Stores, almost certainly the first photographic business in western China. The profits were invested back into the Quaker school, but a committee in London soon disapproved of the venture and it was closed down in 1902.

Missionaries also played a significant role in improving social conditions in western China, including campaigning against opium use, promoting hygiene and, particularly the Quakers, campaigning against, militarism. At a time of increasing hostilities between the local and foreign communities, missionaries also played an important role in bridging the gap between communities, through non-overtly religious organisations such as the YMCA which brought people together to discuss topical issues of the day.

By the end of the first decade of the 20th century, there was growing agitation in Britain about the opium trade in China, and an Imperial Edict against the drug in China. Under pressure, the British government undertook to reduce the imports of opium from India by one-tenth each year, while the Chinese ordered the progressive elimination of opium growing within China, and forbade its use by all government officials and all citizens under the age of 60.

These developments made missionaries feel that they had not done enough to combat the drug: they had treated smokers in hospitals and dispensaries, they had refused to allow them into the church, but they had never conducted a sustained campaign against it.

This the Quakers began in Chungking in 1906, collaborating as far as they could with the Chinese authorities. The inaugural meeting of the Anti-Opium League was held in the Friends Meeting House, with 4 other local missions, the county magistrate and a representative of the Taotai present. The main purpose was to encourage the Taotai to publicise the Imperial Edict – edicts disapproved of by local officials could often be quietly ignored. A larger meeting was held in January 1907 in one of the city's guildhalls, attended by over 1500 people, and another in Chengdu with a keynote speech by Secretary of the British Anti-Opium Society, JG Alexander, attended by over 4000.

The campaign had considerable success: by the end of 1907 there were reportedly only 96 opium dens in Chungking compared with over 900 two years before. The cultivation of opium in the province declined, and fields that had for years been white with poppies reverted to other, more beneficial crops. By 1911 hardly a single opium field could be found in Sichuan.

The foundation of the International Friends Institute in Chungking (or Te Yu Se, the Society for the Advancement of Virtue) in 1907, based on the International Institute in Shanghai, was another notable achievement. A social club whose aim was to foster friendly relations between Chinese and foreigners, it was the brainchild of Quaker Warburton who had grown a little tired of the everyday struggles of missionary work.

At that time in Chungking foreigners had no social contact with Chinese officials and merchants: Warburton hoped that a Friends' Institute would remedy this. His first ally was a local banker Tan Pao-san, who had already given money to the Quakers for a cemetery. Warburton asked him if he would refurnish a building in White Elephant Street in a style that would attract wealthy local people such as himself to attend. Here in October 1909 the International Friends Institute opened.

Membership gradually increased through personal contact and invitation. English classes were arranged which attracted some younger businessmen, but fortnightly lectures proved one of the most popular activities. To keep numbers manageable, attendance was by invitation only, but by the end of 1910 over one hundred people were regularly turning up to hear, for example, the Director of the new Electric Light Works give a talk on the benefits of electricity, or Dr Lo, who had studied some Western medicine in Shanghai, talking about x-rays and hygiene, and alarming his interlocutors by recommending cold baths.

Soon the Institute was open every evening, except Sundays, for lectures, games, reading and conversation. In the reading room there were newspapers, a small exhibition of machinery, and a model of St Paul's Cathedral. The library contained books ranging from the Bible to Sherlock Holmes, Political Economy and Ancient History. Some gymnastics apparatus was put in the recreation room and ping pong made an early appearance as an instrument of sino-western friendship. Alcohol and gambling were strictly forbidden. The Institute was intended to be a counter-balance to other aspects of western culture that were making an appearance in Chungking at that time: the cinema, the theatre, which had just imported a hundred dancing girls from Shanghai on the newly opened steamer service, and some dubious restaurants "where all kinds of wickedness take place daily"[cxxiii]

Many foreigners in the city – Consuls, businessmen, commissioners of customs, naval officers – joined the institute. For most, it was the first opportunity they had had to meet Chinese of their own class. Previously the innate prejudice of most of them had fed on encounters with boatmen and coolies anxious to squeeze as much money as they could out of the foreigner; now they met with men who were educated, courteous and civilised and a habit of informal contact developed which it was hoped could only improve international feeling.

The institute was founded at a key historical moment which gave it a unique position in Chungking. By 1911 as the growing Railway League agitation brought trade almost to a halt, many local and foreign merchants had time on their hands, which they often spent at the Institute building. The institute became one of the most reliable sources of news at a time full of rumour, and this attracted even more people through its doors. It made Warburton the most informed foreigner in the city.

When the revolution came to Chungking on 22 November 1911, while other foreigners took refuge on gunboats on the river, Warburton and his family felt sufficiently protected by his contacts that he remained in the city and was able to watch events at close quarters. As the white flag of the revolution went up over the city, Warburton walked out to see what was happening. There was a cheerful holiday atmosphere on the streets and people, he was pleased to note, greeted him warmly. There was no sign of hostilities.

A few days later, Warburton was granted an audience with the two young men who had emerged as leaders of the city. Warburton was not impressed, but his visit was a great compliment to the leaders: he was their first foreign contact and he became the only foreigner to have a pass to let him go through the city gates after dark.

The Consuls kept their distant from the new regime, not wanting to imply recognition of a rebellious and probably temporary government. Warburton acted as a go-between for the British government in these circumstances. Several years later Consul Brown wrote an article for a Quaker publication praising the Institute as *"beyond doubt the most powerful instrument for good at the present time in West China... I would gladly see a similar institute in every Treaty Port of China."*

The Institute later expanded to larger premises, such was its popularity. The new 3 storey building, paid for by its members, contained a lecture room large enough for 400 people as well as a library, games room, museum and reception rooms. There was a reception for Institute members and their wives, believed to be the first such mixed social occasion in West China.

The contrast between the socially confident Chinese men and their largely illiterate wives with bound feet was stark. Eighty per cent of Chinese women at that time were thought to suffer from TB; opium smoking and suicide were also common. Of all people, they had been the most inaccessible to missionaries, and thus to any outside influence. But as the merchants of the Institute came into contact with western women, educated, active and sharing their husbands' interests, they themselves saw the need for change, and suggested that the Institute should do something to help.

Shortly afterwards the Quakers founded a Women's Institute. It had only two small rooms, but there were classes in domestic science, childcare, needlework and laundry. Outside there was a courtyard where, if their feet allowed them, the women could improve their health by playing badminton. The Women's institute never operated on more than a small scale: during World War I it closed down; it reopened in 1919 with great ambitions, but lack of finance and personnel meant that these were never realised. But gradually during those years more women came along with their husbands to Institute functions.

The institute continued to play a strong role in Chungking society for several years to come. A Hygiene Society was founded there in 1912 and included amongst its members the City Police Chief. It printed and circulated thousands of posters on subjects like "consumption" and "malaria" and ran an essay competition on "How to make Chungking a clean city". The results of the latter were however disappointing: only 5 out of the 35 essays received were deemed acceptable – "probably most people think the conditions are unalterable".

Later they tried to persuade the authorities to build a waterworks – all water was still being carried up from the Yangtze river in buckets – which would help to improve sanitation and firefighting dramatically. But this was beyond the powers, or interests, of such authorities as existed in the city at that time. The Institute did what it could independently, for example, posting notices explaining the causes of cholera and how to avoid infection. They also engaged a woman to visit the homes of the illiterate. In 1923 there was a campaign against flies, supported by placards, lectures in the streets illustrated with twelve-inch models of flies, and thousands of flytraps sold at cost price.

In 1913 the Institute petitioned the authorities for the opening of a public park, but without success. It was not until 1918 that the Institute bought a piece of land to use as a sports ground and was able to start its own football team. The institute campaigned for reforestation, and introduced the eucalyptus tree to the city and there was soon great demand for this fast-growing tree to provide much-needed shade from the Sichuan sun. In 1914 work started on a boys' orphanage, which four years later had over 100 occupants. A girls' orphanage followed.

In 1915 the Institute raised money for relief work in Poland and Serbia – it now had 500 members of fourteen different nationalities.

In 1920 Chungking suffered one of its periodic fires and the Institute collected money to help the homeless. Members made efforts to raise awareness of the need for prison reform, visiting local prisons and being appalled by their conditions; and pushed for the opening of a kindergarten in the city, run along Montessori lines. Although the kindergarten was only open intermittently, as it proved difficult to find a suitable teacher, it is claimed to be the first example of organised infant education in the whole of western China.

In 1917 the institute held a particularly interesting exhibition which contrasted the natural resources of China with the low level of their exploitation. Charts demonstrated that China had the largest coal reserves in the world but the lowest level of production. Maps contrasted railways in Germany and Szechwan – not a line had yet been laid in the latter.[cxxiv]

Through collaboration between foreigners and locals in all of these activities, the suspicion of the foreigner and his religion was gradually eroded. By 1922, over four thousand people were visiting the premises of the Institute every month and it enjoyed great prestige within the city. But from 1922 onwards, the Institute began to face increased competition from a rival establishment – the YMCA – set up in Chungking's Guild Hall by American Bob Service.

The YMCA organised and participated in similar community events as the Quakers. This included a series of lectures on economic and social issues of the age, such as "The Advantages of Railways", "Comparison of Hand Labour and Machinery" and "The Origin of Society". It then developed an even more ambitious plan to set up a Trade School to start teaching a whole range of modern industrial techniques, including the manufacture of paper, cement, textiles and steel, and road building, irrigation, salt refining, milling and electricity generation. But a promise of funding for the venture from America never materialised and the project faulted badly, for a time damaging the YMCA's reputation.

More success was a hygiene campaign which led to the distribution of 19,700 tracts, calendars and posters containing information about the dangers of flies, fleas, mosquitoes and spitting. The organising committee took a stall at the Spring Flower festival at a local temple and gave public lectures on personal and public hygiene.

As modern day visitors to western China will testify, there is still some way to go in convincing locals of the dangers of spitting, but clearly progress has been made in the other fields described. The contribution of the Britons described here to the advancement of knowledge of China in the outside world, as well as to the development of western China, has been immense.

Chapter 7:

<u>The end of an era</u>
<u>– and the start of a new one</u>

Modern day Chongqing: confluence of the Yangtze and Jialing rivers, Chaotianmen district

This chapter looks at the end of the colonial era and the decline of British influence in western China. It also considers the reversal of roles of sorts, as China's policymakers look to expand China's own economic influence beyond its own borders to the west, using the city of Chongqing as its catalyst, just as the British planned 150 years previously.

But even as China's economic might has grown enormously in the last 150 years, the western China of today still retains many of the characteristics described by the British explorers in this book.

It is this stark juxtaposition between the past, present and future, which all seem to be happening simultaneous in much of China, that made my experience of Chongqing so confusing, surprising, intoxicating, frustrating and ultimately unforgettable. I will also look at the lasting legacy of British influence in western China and the visible traces of the treaty port era that remain.

Ultimately, western China did not live up to the expectations of colonial expansionists. Only 3 percent of British overseas investments in 1914 were located in China, despite the lofty predictions of what the opening up of inland China would do for British industry.

The opening up of western China to trade was severely hindered, amongst other things, by war, social upheaval and the poverty and self-sufficiency of the native population.

There was also a reluctance on the part of the big British commercial players of the time to take the risk of investing substantially in western China when they were doing quite well for themselves on the eastern seaboard. This left western China to the smaller, more risk-friendly British entrepreneurs such as Archibald Little, but the likes of Little did not have the financial power to exploit opportunities to the full.

With hindsight, there was no solid commercial basis for Western China providing an expanding market for British industry during the late nineteenth and early twentieth centuries.

There were some early signs that all was not going quite to plan. Writing as early as 1882, Oxenham, British Consul in Chinkiang wrote:

'*The present stagnant condition of foreign trade in China requires consideration. The chief reason for this stagnation state of things is, I understand, that the great body of the people, the poorer and agricultural classes, do not buy our manufactures, the purchase of them being mainly confined to the richer, middle, and trading classes. The poor complain that our cotton goods wear out too quickly (in two years); that the thread of which they are composed is weak..The native cloth is cheaper, stouter, and stronger'.*^{cxxv}

Westerners also underestimated the difficulty of obtaining access to the Chinese market where trade was dominated by middlemen, guilds and corrupt officials. The Times concluded in 1892 that: *"so far, the general conditions of the trade of Chungking have not been altered by the opening of the port to foreign trade; the distribution still remains wholly in the hands of native merchants, and the carrying trade as it was. Without steamers, insurance or a foreign bank, the present system is not likely to be disturbed"*^{cxxvi}

And finally, history was against the success of Chungking as a treaty port. Its late opening to foreign trade, compared with other treaty ports in China, meant that it did not have the time to establish itself properly before the series of tumultuous political changes happening in China at the time took hold. Steam shipping only appeared in 1909, a few years before the disruptions of the republican revolution and the First World War. Westerners placed great hopes in the commercial transformation effected by steam and the arrival of the first foreign banking. Unfortunately for them, these developments coincided with the destructive parasitism of the warlord. Sichuan was especially fractious in this respect. Added to this, the serious geographical challenges of reaching Chungking and the connected financial risks, and this often tipped the balance against investment[cxxvii].

As we saw earlier in this book, most Britons living in Chungking were chased out of the country following the Communist Revolution in 1949. Lives were made very difficult for those few who chose to remain. Western contact with China was all but cut off between the early 1950s and late 70s during the difficult periods of the Great Leap Forward and Cultural Revolution. In global terms, China became an inconsequential backwater during this period, neglected by the world and turned inward on itself.

So what became of the Western and particularly British influence on the city during these years?

The Chongqing of today is a thoroughly Chinese city. But not the kind of China I was expecting to find from the reading I had done before going there. Where were the 5000 years of history? The traditional Taoist harmony between man and nature? Or any visible traces of traditional Chinese architecture and culture for that matter?

The Chongqing of today is one of the fastest growing cities in the world. Its location, at the confluence of the Yangtze and Jialing rivers remains just as impressive today as it did to early western travellers arriving upstream. Today, the wooden hovels which once littered the shoreline have been replaced by a growing army of steel and glass skyscrapers, pushing ever further into the sky. Where once no wheeled transport was able to penetrate, the city centre becomes ever more gridlocked as, it is estimated, 1300 new cars are added to the city's streets per day.

But behind this facade of modernity, the old Chongqing is ever present, in many ways little unchanged from the 19th century city described in this book.

Penetrating the communities which line the steep banks of the central Yuzhong district down to the rivers on either side, one is still transported back into Dickensian times. These communities remain linked by flights of stone steps. Many live in flimsy, makeshift wooden houses with little light, sanitation and ventilation. Every day activities – cooking, washing and socialising - take place rather outside, in view of all. These streets are filthy and the smells all too often nauseating.

This is what struck me most when reading the records of life in the city quoted in this book. While much in fast changing in China, there is also much that is stagnant. While the media may report that China's tiger economy is taking over the world, flooding our shops with cheap imports and buying up western debt to keep our economies afloat, this is only a small part of a bigger story, and the world I saw in Chongqing did not equate very well with that.

Inland Chinese cities still have a long way to go before they rival the level of economic development and sophistication of Shanghai and Beijing, never mind Hong Kong and Singapore. And it is this huge and growing gap in levels of development that makes China's future path so interesting. I often described my sorties in Chongqing as "three centuries in one day". On a visit to the countryside, you might stretch that to three or four!

History, or more precisely the preservation of it, is of little interest to the modern Chinese. With such a rush to modernise, combined with China's recent past where everything that was old was seen as bad, history is of little value. This can be seen in the rampant destruction of a large part of Beijing's traditional housing in the form of its hutong, or a campaign during my time in Chongqing to raise large parts of the historical centre to make way for high rise towers and roads. Modern Chongqing is expanding at a rate of approximately 30 km2 per year – maps need to be reprinted every 3 months so fast is the growth.

Traces of Chungking's treaty port past are therefore difficult to find for the casual visitor, and are threatened by this push for modernisation. Many European-style buildings were also damaged during the city's extensive bombing by the Japanese during the Second World War. But take a bit of time and with a bit of research you can still see the Consulates of Canada, Belgium... on a ridge of hills in thick undergrowth along the south bank of the Yangtze.

Some are inhabited by migrant workers, packed into their once handsome rooms. At the former Canadian consulate building, I came upon a migrant worker going about his ablutions in an outside trough, perhaps once used for watering the Consulate's manicured gardens.

Walking along a higher ridge of these hills one day, I came across a line of impressive Victorian family houses, now abandoned. If I was going to spend more time living in Chungking, that would be the kind of environment I would choose to live in – high above the bustling city below, surrounded by nature. It brought the stories of the missionaries in their summer houses in the hills to life – you could see exactly why they chose to live there and that life during those summer months can't have been so bad for them. I dreamt of finding in particular the missionary house with a swimming pool – such a decadent symbol of a bygone age - but alas, either undergrowth or the locals had got the better of it.

The Friends Boys School still goes strong and is one of the few old colonial buildings that displays its history with some pride.

Although the main old school building was destroyed by Red Guards in the 1960s, a smaller building and the Headmaster's house still remain. The corridors of the newer school building are lined with old photographs from the time of the Davidsons described in this book. The old school bell, won from British warship HMS x after they were defeated by the school boys in a football match, survives and is used several times per day to signal the start and end of class.

Two separate British Embassy buildings survive – the earlier one in the centre of the city, and the later one in the hills on the south bank of the Yangtze. Both are still in fairly good condition, now dedicated to more mundane uses. The former is now home to a packing company and overshadowed by ugly, decaying tenement buildings. The Embassy tennis court described in historic documents obviously fell victim to these encroaching residences. The later occupies one of the best positions in Chongqing, on the highest ridge of the mountains south of the river.

A one storey building in a mixture of British and Chinese styles, it has patio doors which lead out onto a terrace – once used for Embassy receptions, such as when the young

Prince George visited wartime Chungking in 1926 – and then onto a grassy garden with spectacular views over the city. The build now houses one of the city's hundreds of hotpot restaurants – the Chungking's speciality which consists of a boiling vat of chilli oil into which you add meat, vegetables, congealed blood, frogs, brains… whatever takes your fancy.

There is also the former residence of British Ambassador to Chungking during the war years, Sir Archibald Kerr – the most difficult of the vestiges of British history in Chungking to find. Scrambling through brambles, down slopes and through deep undergrowth I finally came across a small bungalow hidden deep in the woods. Now inhabited by a migrant worker, the bungalow retained its handsome louvered shutters and ornate fireplace. There was even an antique Chinese-style four poster bed, perhaps once used by Ambassador Kerr himself. It was difficult to ascertain what the migrant worker, in his thick Sichuan accent was trying to tell me, for I understood that Chiang Kai Shek had once lived there and he had offered its use to the British Ambassador of the time so I knew I was in the right place.

Archibald Little's home on the riverfront still stands proud, and is an architectural gem – a mixture of western and Chinese styles – and one of the oldest western structures left in town.

One day I managed to gain access to it, thanks to a friendly guard, scrambling through an abandoned police station to gain access to the back of the house. Apart from a few rotting floorboards and half-collapsed outhouses the building is in remarkably good condition, and its elegant curving staircase, carved wooden panels and expansive river terrace contrast sharply with your average modern Chinese apartment block. It was later used for a time as an officers' club for the United States Yangtze Patrol when they had a gunboat in port. In recent years, there has been much talk of local property developers wanting to acquire the building and convert it into an exclusive gentleman's club, but this has yet to occur.

The average lifespan of a building in today's Chongqing is an incredible 10 years (20 years for the rest of China), before it is knocked down and built again – an important factor is sustaining the incredible GDP growth rates of 15% or more that western Chinese provinces regularly see.

One building which has fared much better than the rest is the former home of the French Marines in Chungking on the Yangtze water front (above).

Several years ago this was restored and transformed into a "French" restaurant known as the "Champs Elysees". The building is wonderful with a galleried courtyard that even contains a small museum of the foreign history of Chungking (all in Chinese). The main building has been fairly sympathetically restored and has a wonderful wraparound terrace looking out onto the river. I recommend it for the atmosphere; not for the pseudo-French food…

Western influence in western China is of course not what it was. Since Deng Xiaoping transformed China's economy with his opening up and reform policies, China is no longer the economically weak backwater it once was. As China has grown economically, so foreign interest in the country has increased again, both as a source of cheap labour to manufacture goods more cheaply than in the west, and also as a market for western products.

This trend is certainly more marked in eastern and southern China, but it also growing in its western reaches. Over 50 years after it had closed, the British government reopened its Consulate in Chongqing in 2000 to build on the increasing British interest and opportunities in the region, and this is where I spent 3 years working between 2007 and 2010.

But life for foreigners in western China continues to be difficult and a world away from the cosmopolitan cities of Beijing, Shanghai or even Guangzhou. The foreign population of Chongqing today is estimated at approximately 1000, out of a city population of 9 million – mainly businessmen or intrepid English teachers, including a substantial number of "modern day missionaries", preaching the word of God through their teaching work. The limited number of foreigners means they still attract some of the unwanted attention described in this book, albeit without the animosity of the past, which becomes even worst once you leave the city limits.

For these reasons and more, doing business in the West remains more difficult than elsewhere in the Middle Kingdom: many western businesses try and fail. The case of British businessman Neil Hayward, found dead in a Chongqing hotel in 2011 after getting mixed up in the business affairs of wealthy Communist party officials including former trade minister and Chongqing Party Secretary Bo Xilai, is an extreme example of the continuing difficulties – and occasionally the dangers – of doing business in China.

China remains to this day largely self-sufficient for the needs of its population. What it wants from the outside world it picks and chooses, and increasingly it takes the technology it wants only to manufacture near copies at lower prices.

And today Chongqing itself is reaching outward. Hopes are being placed on it by the Chinese themselves, rather than external forces, to open up western China and become an economic growth pole of the region, rather like the role of Chicago in opening up the centre and west of the United States in the nineteenth century. My role as Political Consul at the British Consulate-General was to follow and report back to London this development, and spot opportunities for British co-operation with western China as it faced the challenges of "opening up and reform".

During my time in Chongqing, there was renewed interest within political circles in Britain in inland China. The city received visits by David Cameron and George Osborne – at the time leaders of the opposition; David Miliband as Foreign Secretary; Alastair Darling as Chancellor; and John Hutton as Secretary of State for Trade. The BBC did a series of reports on the rampant development of this city that the west had never heard of. And the Chinese government propaganda machine went into overdrive on the prospects for the development of western China as a whole that Chongqing's growth pole status was going to bring about.

As Guangzhou/Shenzhen was to south-east China in the 1980s, and Shanghai to East China in the 1990s, Chongqing is expected to play the leading role for a rapid development of western China in the early 21st century.

It became China's fourth municipality in 1997 and encompasses the huge, and controversial, Three Gorges Dam Project. The Chinese government has ambitious plans to make Chongqing a transport hub of western China linking it to surrounding regions and further afield, including Western Europe.

Many commentators say China's ability to develop westward has always hindered its development and prevented it from fully copying America's successful "Go West" policy. The railways and roads linking Western China to the outside world that colonial expansionists dreamed of so many years before are now becoming a reality, as Chongqing seeks to develop transport and trade routes to the sea in 8 different directions.

In June 2011 the first cargo train from Chongqing to western Europe started out on its 11,000 kilometre journey across Kazakhstan, Russia, Belarus and Poland to Germany, cutting the travel time for cargo from 36 days by container ship from Shanghai or Guangzhou, to just 13 days [cxxviii]. Just as once the West dreamt of flooding the west of China with its products, Chongqing now dreams of the same. As well as being Asia's biggest manufacturer of motorbikes and a major automotive centre, the Chongqing government has ambitious plans to make the city the biggest manufacturer of laptop computers in the world. In the first five months of 2011, Chongqing sold 2.43 million laptop computers abroad - 20 percent of the city's total exports.

In general, China's interests in Europe are growing fast. Between 2008 and 2010 Chinese direct investment in Europe multiplied six fold, and the pace is growing. China is slowly and discreetly acquiring stakes in key infrastructure installations (the ports of Piraeus in Greece, Naples in Italy, energy companies such as Total), and key areas of manufacturing such as the automotive industry (acquisitions of MG Rover in the UK, and Volvo in Sweden), building material suppliers (such as Cifa in Italy and Gandara Censa in Spain) and even perfumes and French vineyards. The pace of growth of these investments is causing some concern about the sheer economic might of China, fuelled by over-enthusiastic media reporting.

But these concerns should be kept in perspective, at least for the time being. In reality only 2% of foreign direct investment into Europe currently comes from China, dwarfing investments from places such as the United States and Japan. But if you include investment from Hong Kong and those transiting through tax havens and other shell companies with links to China, the total weight of Chinese-linked investments in Europe could already be as high as 20%.

Whichever way you look at it, as Napoleon once predicted, the Chinese dragon is awakening and beginning to shake the world.

Many of the commentators on western China's development cited in this book said that when western China was ready, it would develop on its own terms. All were proved largely right. Where the west once thought it could rescue China from its backwardness with its technological prowess and know-how, China now assesses European countries as being in decline and needing China to get them out of the mess they have got themselves into – through trade and debt bailouts. The tables have turned and a power shift in the world to the east has begun.

But the British pioneers in a foreign far-off land described in this book were important precursors to that process and had an impact on it: in botany, in education, science, medicine and religion. As many of the tales recounted in this book demonstrate, western China also had a lasting impact on them, in both good and bad ways – just as it had on me.

This book stands as a record of western China's European past and the men and women that formed it.

Footnotes

Chapter 1: Introduct on

---

[i] Across China on foot: Edwin Dingle

Chapter 2: Trade

[ii] No Dogs and Not Many Chinese: Treaty Port Life in China, *1843-1943*: Frances Wood (John Murray, 2000)

[iii] National Maritime Museum, Greenwich exhibition on trade with China

[iv] For all the tea in China – Sarah Rose

[v] Three years in Western China - Alexander Hosie

[vi] Through the Yangtze Gorges – Archibald Little, P6

[vii] Across China on foot – Edwin Dingle

[viii] Across China on foot – Edwin Dingle

[ix] Mad about the Mekong: Exploration and Empire in South-east Asia – John Keay (2005)

[x] quoted from The Times, 2 Dec 1869

[xi] Across China on foot – Edwin Dingle, P45

[xii] Across China on foot – Edwin Dingle, P 111

[xiii] "The Union Jack on the Upper Yangzi: The Treaty Port of Chongqing: 1891 – 1943": James J. Matthews – York University,

Canada graduate thesis

xiv Through the Yangtze Gorges – Archibald Little, P 111 – 112

xv Through the Yangtze Gorges – Archibald Little, P 115

xvi The Times, 26 Feb 1887: The Upper Yang-Tse as a Trade Route (from a correspondent)

xvii Friends to China: The Davidson Brothers and the Friends'

Mission to China 1886 – 1939 – Charles Tyzack

xviii Three years in Western China - Alexander Hosie

xix Three years in Western China - Alexander Hosie

xx China and salt made the world go round: http://www.salt.org.il/frame_china1.html

xxi http://www.willysthomas.net/Butterfield&Swire.htm

xxii Across China on foot – Edwin Dingle

xxiii Land and River routes to western China – A.D Blue

Chapter 3: Diplomacy

xxiv China Consuls – P.D Coates P 307

xxv China Consuls – P.D Coates

xxvi China Consuls – P.D Coates

xxvii Travels and Researches in Western China - Baber

xxviii "The Union Jack on the Upper Yangzi: The Treaty Port of Chongqing, 1891 – 1943" – James J. Matthews, York university Canada graduate thesis

xxix Through the Yangtze Gorges – Archibald Little

xxx China Consuls – P.D Coates

xxxi China Consuls – P.D Coates, P 306

xxxii China Consuls – P.D Coates, P 307

xxxiii China Consuls – P.D Coates, P x307

xxxiv China Consuls – P.D Coates, P 420

xxxv Friends to China: The Davidson Brothers and the Friends' Mission to Chinam 1886 – 1939 – Charles Tyzack

xxxvi The Times, 9 June 1941

xxxvii Chungking Diary - Robert Payne – P 32-33

xxxviii The Long Road back to China – Carl Crow, P8

xxxix China Consuls – P.D Coates, P313

Chapter 4: Lifestyle and Culture

xl Intimate China: The Chinese as I have seen then – Alicia Little, P5

[xli] Alicia Little, as quoted in Wise Daughters from Foreign Lands – Elisabeth Croll, P 26

[xlii] On a Chinese Screen – Somerset Maugham, P 147 - 148

[xliii] Through the Yangtze Gorges – Archibald Little, P 244

[xliv] Friends to China: The Davidson Brothers and the Friends' Mission to China 1886 – 1939 – Charles Tyzack

[xlv] On a Chinese Screen – Somerset Maugham, P 149

[xlvi] On a Chinese Screen – Somerset Maugham, P 147

[xlvii] China Consuls – P.D Coates, P 306

[xlviii] Intimate China: the Chinese as I have seen them – Alicia Little, P89

[xlix] Golden Inches – Grace Service

[l] Friends to China: The Davidson Brothers and the Friends' Mission to China 1886 – 1939 – Charles Tyzack, P 142

[li] Golden Inches – Grace Service, P 269

[lii] Across China on foot – Edwin Dingle, P 41

[liii] Through the Yangtze Gorges – Archibald Little, P 217

[liv] Through the Yangtze Gorges – Archibald Little, P 234

[lv] The Yangtze Valley and Beyond - Isabella Bird, P 296

lvi Through the Yangtze Gorges – Archibald Little, P 306

lvii Across China on foot – Edwin Dingle, P 24

lviii The Yangtze Valley and Beyond – Isabella Bird, P 328

lix The Yangtze Valley and Beyond – Isabella Bird, P 217

lx The Yangtze Valley and Beyond – Isabella Bird, P 246

lxi The Yangtze Valley and Beyond – Isabella Bird, P 206

lxii Across China on foot – Edwin Dingle, P 152

lxiii The Yangtze Valley and Beyond – Isabella Bird, P 206

lxiv Intimate China: The Chinese as I have seen them – Alicia Little, P 82

lxv Intimate China: The Chinese as I have seen them – Alicia Little, P 86

lxvi Golden Inches – Grace Service – P71

lxvii The Yangtze Valley and Beyond – Isabella Bird, P 206

lxviii Through the Yangtze Gorges – Archibald Little, P 248

lxix Through the Yangtze Gorges – Archibald Little, P 265

lxx Intimate China: The Chinese as I have seen then – Alicia Little, P 139

lxxi Intimate China: The Chinese as I have seen them – Alicia Little, P 143

lxxii Intimate China: The Chinese as I have seen them – Alicia Little,

P 151

[lxxiii] Intimate China: The Chinese as I have seen them – Alicia Little, P 156

[lxxiv] Wise Daughters from Foreign Lands – Elisabeth Croll, P 56

[lxxv] Chungking Diary - Robert Payne, P 114

[lxxvi] Chungking Diary - Robert Payne, P 265

[lxxvii] Journal of the Royal Asiatic Society Hong Kong Branch – Paul Bolding

[lxxviii] Chungking Diary - Robert Payne, P 265

[lxxix] Chungking Diary - Robert Payne, P 459

Chapter 5: Religion and Education

[lxxx] Friends to China: The Davidson Brothers and the Friends'

Mission to China 1886 – 1939 – Charles Tyzack,

[lxxxi] Friends to China: The Davidson Brothers and the Friends' Mission to China 1886 – 1939 – Charles Tyzack, P 10-11

[lxxxii] Friends to China: The Davidson Brothers and the Friends'

Mission to China 1886 – 1939 – Charles Tyzack

[lxxxiii] Friends to China: The Davidson Brothers and the Friends' Mission to China 1886 – 1939 – Charles Tyzack, P 28

lxxxiv The Yangtze Valley and Beyond – Isabella Bird, P 172

lxxxv Friends to China: The Davidson Brothers and the Friends'

Mission to China 1886 – 1939 – Charles Tyzack, P 323

lxxxvi Intimate China: The Chinese as I have seen them – Alicia Little, P 233-234

lxxxvii Friends to China: The Davidson Brothers and the Friends' Mission to China 1886 – 1939 – Charles Tyzack, P 18

lxxxviii Friends to China: The Davidson Brothers and the Friends' Mission to China 1886 – 1939 – Charles Tyzack, P 20

lxxxix Friends to China: The Davidson Brothers and the Friends' Mission to China 1886 – 1939 – Charles Tyzack, P 89

xc Friends to China: The Davidson Brothers and the Friends' Mission to China 1886 – 1939 – Charles Tyzack, P 28

xci Friends to China: The Davidson Brothers and the Friends' Mission to China 1886 – 1939 – Charles Tyzack, P 41

xcii Friends to China: The Davidson Brothers and the Friends' Mission to China 1886 – 1939 – Charles Tyzack, P 53

xciii Friends to China: The Davidson Brothers and the Friends' Mission to China 1886 – 1939 – Charles Tyzack, P 54

xciv Friends to China: The Davidson Brothers and the Friends' Mission to China 1886 – 1939 – Charles Tyzack, P 27

xcv Friends to China: The Davidson Brothers and the Friends'

Mission to China 1886 – 1939 – Charles Tyzack, P 76

xcvi Friends to China: The Davidson Brothers and the Friends' Mission to China 1886 – 1939 – Charles Tyzack, P 132

xcvii Golden Inches – Grace Service – P267

xcviii Golden Inches – Grace Service – P271

xcix Friends to China: The Davidson Brothers and the Friends' Mission to China 1886 – 1939 – Charles Tyzack, P 168

c Friends to China: The Davidson Brothers and the Friends' Mission to China 1886 – 1939 – Charles Tyzack, P 143

ci Friends to China: The Davidson Brothers and the Friends' Mission to China 1886 – 1939 – Charles Tyzack, P 184

cii Friends to China: The Davidson Brothers and the Friends' Mission to China 1886 – 1939 – Charles Tyzack, P 185

ciii Friends to China: The Davidson Brothers and the Friends' Mission to China 1886 – 1939 – Charles Tyzack, P 189

civ Friends to China: The Davidson Brothers and the Friends' Mission to China 1886 – 1939 – Charles Tyzack, P 190

cv Foreign Office report, 1951

cvi Friends to China: The Davidson Brothers and the Friends' Mission to China 1886 – 1939 – Charles Tyzack, P 205

cvii Society for Anglo-Chinese Understanding (SACU) report

Chapter 6: Science

[cviii] Across China on foot – Edwin Dingle

[cix] The Man who Loved China – Simon Winchester, P 71-72

[cx] The Man who Loved China – Simon Winchester, P80

[cxi] The Man who Loved China – Simon Winchester, P 92

[cxii] Science and Civilisation, Vol. VII, Part 2 – Joseph Needham

[cxiii] The Man who Loved China – Joseph Needham, P 188

[cxiv] The Man who Loved China – Simon Winchester, P 157

[cxv] The Man who Loved China – Simon Winchester, P 166

[cxvi] For all the tea in China – Sarah Rose, P 1-2

[cxvii] http://www.hadland.me.uk/gill/gill5.html

[cxviii] The River at the centre of the World – Simon Winchester

[cxix] Journal of the Royal Asiatic Society Hong Kong Branch Vol. 43 (ISSN 1991-7295196)

[cxx] For all the tea in China – Sarah Rose, P 129

[cxxi] George Forrest - Wikipedia

[cxxii] Royal Botanic Gardens, Kew official website

[cxxiii] Friends to China: The Davidson Brothers and the Friends' Mission to China 1886 – 1939 – Charles Tyzack, P 100-102

[cxxiv] Friends to China: The Davidson Brothers and the Friends'

Chapter 7: The End of an era.. and the start of a new one

[cxxv] China Consuls – P.D Coates

[cxxvi] The Trade of Chungking – The Times, 18 August 1892

[cxxvii] "The Union Jack on the Upper Yangzi: The Treaty Port of Chongqing: 1891 – 1943" – James J. Matthews, York University, Canada graduate thesis

[cxxviii] China Daily, 2 July 2011

Printed in Great Britain
by Amazon.co.uk, Ltd.,
Marston Gate.